St. Joseph Writers Guild: An Anthology

Edited by Julie L. Casey
and Donna Whittaker

Amazing Things Press

Edited by Julie L. Casey and Donna Whittaker
Book design by Julie L. Casey

ISBN 978-0692222843
Second edition 2014
Published by The St. Joseph Writers Guild,
St. Joseph, Missouri

ABOUT THE ST. JOSEPH WRITERS GUILD
By Jill Perkins, guild historian

The St. Joseph Writers Guild has had a long history in St. Joseph, Missouri. Prior to the 1950s, Creative Writers were a part of the St. Joseph Art League. They shared their passion for the arts with many who pioneered the arts movement in St. Joseph. There were renowned names in the group, such as Wall, Geiger, Herzog, Tootle, Kirkpatrick, Welch, and Wyeth. The roster read like a "who's who" of modern elite St. Joseph society.

In the 1950s, the writers guild was a branch of the National League of American Pen Women in Washington, D.C. We made a name for ourselves by hosting local, state, and regional meetings in St. Joseph. Two of our writers served as president of the Missouri chapter. Many of our chapter members received notable awards for their writing.

In 1979 the St. Joseph branch disbanded from the National League of American Pen Women in order to join an organization with a base that was closer to home, the Missouri Writers Guild. Many of our local members served as state board members, held state offices, and accumulated numerous awards over the years for their writing skills.

Today the St. Joseph Writers Guild has a heart for writing and for writers. We encourage anyone who writes, or who thinks they might like to write, to seek us out. We respect all people; all are welcome, from every creed, social standing, and even age. We have had members from the ripe age of eleven years old to the ripe old age of 90+. Our youngest member was 11-year-old Mary Margaret Trapp. She was a much-published author in the early 1960s. Creative writing knows no limits or boundaries.

The goal of the St. Joseph Writers Guild is to encourage writers to have confidence in themselves and their writing ability. We wish to promote in them the desire to further develop their skills. It is our task to promote respect and enthusiasm for the written word.

This anthology of some of our guild members' works is a written collage of our passions for the art of creative writing. This collection will now be preserved for future generations. Long after we writers are gone, this book of our written words will live on. In the future, as this book pops up again and again, it will be like looking backward and seeing the footprint we made in the sands of time.

Persons interested in writing are **always welcome** to visit the St. Joseph Writers' Guild meetings. Meetings are held at the Joyce Raye Patterson Senior Citizens Center, 100 South 10th Street, St. Joseph, Missouri, on the third Saturday of each month (except second Saturday in August) beginning at 1:00 p.m. Free parking is on the lower level.

There is a short meeting, frequent guest speakers, occasional take home challenges, and a workshop period when members share what they have written. Members share constructive comments and suggest markets where writings may be submitted.

TABLE OF CONTENTS

CONTRIBUTORS

Patti Bennett

Writing has been an interest of Patti's since her elementary years. She worked on the school newspaper in high school and college. She became a member of the National League of American Pen Women in the 1970s and is currently a member of the St. Joseph Writers Guild. Her first sales were juvenile puzzles, mostly Biblical ones. Since then she has sold poems, children's stories, and articles to various publications. Writing continues to be an exciting interest in her senior years.

Marianne Brachman

Marianne is a social worker who loves to write about her childhood exploring the Midwest. After moving multiple times for job transfers, she and her husband happily call St. Joseph their "forever home". She is a member of the St. Joseph Writers Guild.

Julie L. Casey

Julie L. Casey lives in a rural area near St. Joseph, Missouri, with her husband, Jonn Casey, a science teacher, and their three youngest sons. Julie has Bachelor of Science degrees in education and computer programming and has written four books. She enjoys historical reenacting, wildlife rehabilitation, teaching her children, and writing books that capture the imaginations of young people. She is a member of the Missouri Writers Guild and the St. Joseph Writers Guild.

Jeannetta R. Danford

Jeannetta Danford is a widowed, retired schoolteacher who writes when the mood strikes, generally a remembrance of her own. Her theory is that if it didn't happen to her, it isn't worth writing about. She is a long-time member of the St. Joseph Writer's Guild. Her observations have been published in several national magazines as well as the local newspaper's senior page, "Young at Heart", formerly an eight-page publication, of which she has been the editor since 2006. She reads more than she writes and would like to change that. But probably won't.

Nshan Erganian

Nshan Erganian was born and raised in St. Joseph, Missouri. He is a member of the St. Joseph Writer's Guild. *Keeper of the Mountain* is his first novel. His other writings include the short story *Mom Was A Baseball Legend* and *A Grandparent's Guide to Caring for Twin Toddlers*.

Mary Jane Fields

MARY JANE FIELDS, a former pre-school, kindergarten, and college teacher, is a St. Joseph native. She was a regular contributor to two newspapers, has published two early childhood books, and for 17 years, compiled *Thoughts For*

Early Childhood Teachers, which had subscribers from all 50 states and several foreign countries. Since retiring, she has contributed short stories for two books and now enjoys writing memoirs.

James Fly

James Fly earned his B.A. in journalism from Pacific Union College, Angwin, California. In his career, he has edited both church and college publications as well as two weekly newspapers. His book, *Africa Adopted Us*, is currently being reprinted by Pacific Press. A co-owner of A-Z's FreshAir Fare in downtown St. Joseph, MO., James writes a monthly health column for *The Regular Joe.* He graduated from the Institute for Integration in 2011 as a certified health coach. An avid photographer, he belongs to the Midwest Artists Association and is a founding member of Gallery 7, a cooperative art gallery in downtown St. Joseph. He is a member of the St. Joseph Writers Guild.

Charles Gilliland

Charles Gilliland lives in Troy, Kansas and enjoys writing fiction and how-to articles. He is a member of the St. Joseph Writers Guild.

Jill Perkins

Long before she could speak, Jill Perkins' conscious thoughts spilled out of her mind in the form of rhythm and rhyme. At school, when she became capable of writing words that were legible, her future was never a mystery to her:

she was born to write poetry. She is a member of the St. Joseph Writers Guild and is the immediate past president. As president, she organized the Young Writers Contest to encourage young people to write.

Jan Powell

Jan Powell worked 15 years as a school nurse in the St. Joseph School District. She joined the St. Joseph Writers Guild in 2012 and has found that she enjoys being a part of such a talented group of writers. She believes that everyone has the potential to tell others their story, whether it be a poem, short story, or other form.

Donald E. Sherwood

Donald Sherwood writes poems and song lyrics. He also does historical research articles from time to time. He is a member of the St. Joseph Writers Guild.

Betty Sill

Betty Sill enjoys writing inspirational poetry and short stories. She is a member of the St. Joseph Writers Guild.

Susan Walter

Susan Walter, a long time member of the St. Joseph Writers Guild, is the most published member and the senior member having reached her ninth decade. She is active on the "Young at Heart" editorial staff. She has published entertaining memoirs in the "I am Susan's..."

format in a Lutheran periodical. She also creates word puzzles. A gifted poet and talented artist, Susan is an inspiration. She enjoys her six children, thirteen grandchildren, and six great grandchildren, creative writing, and painting with oils.

Donna Whittaker

Donna Whittaker is a life-long reader and writer. Her senior year in high school she was the Editor of the school yearbook. Writing has been an important part of her employment and volunteering throughout her life. She was the editor of the Myasthenia Gravis Foundation of America newsletter for several years. She has written numerous articles on aspects of living with myasthenia gravis and was one of the first myasthenics to share her experiences by having a website devoted to living with this condition beginning in 1996. She is the author of *W. T. Rawleigh, His Life, His Company and Collectibles 1889-1989* and several "Young at Heart" and "Capper's" articles. She is the current president of the St. Joseph Writers Guild.

Gloria Williams

Gloria Williams has a BA in Education and Sociology from Oklahoma City University and a master's degree in religious education at SMU in Dallas, Texas. Being married to a Methodist pastor, she and her husband were missionaries to Brazil for 12 years. They were honored as distinguished alumni of OCU and Gloria was honored by Rotarians in Savannah, Missouri. She has been a teacher, a legal secretary, bookkeeper, speaker and a free-lance writer. She is a member of the St. Joseph Writers Guild.

SECTION I

Poetry

POETRY FOR SENIORS
By Susan Walter

In my ripe old age of 94,
The age I'm not so "pert,"
I'm grateful for a simple thing —
That wrinkles do not hurt.

I ate my spinach, rich in iron
When suddenly I found,
I could lift my heavy husband
Five feet above the ground.

I used to do aerobics
When I was young and able.
But now I exercise a bit,
While holding on to tables.

God will take me when He's ready,
When the angels sing "Hosanna,"
But I'm just a little skeptical
About buying green bananas.

SWEET SLEEP
By Jeannetta Danford

Awakening, I turned,
Mind-fogged
And sleep sedated,
And raised my head
Above your pillow
To check the time.
In the soft orange glow
Of half-past two a.m.
The silver of your hair
Touched me with surprise.
In the fading wisps
Of a disappearing dream,
You and I were young.

THE SOLITARY PAIR
By James Fly

They walk the same streets
but they will never meet--
this solitary pair.

Their lives have never intersected
for they were never protected
from the holocaust
of human despair:

As a toddler,
he witnessed a murder
and all of his life he's cowered;
in her life as a wife
she was beaten senseless
and so, defenseless,
lives in a castle
with the drawbridge never lowered.

This solitary pair walks the same street
it seems like forever
but never
together........

OLD BARN
By Betty Sill

There she stands on the side of the hill
Her roof caved in,
Her paint nearly peeled;
Her grandeur stands out
From days gone by.
I wonder why, why, why
Should she be left to decay?
In her prime she stored
Up the hay and any old thing
They wanted out of the way.
She's going; it's sheer neglect
She stands there feeble
Begging to be fixed.

"OLD BARN" Photo by Julie L. Casey

TIME
By Julie L. Casey

Time is a bitter old woman
Constantly nagging at her worldly husband,
Complaining that her grown children
Never slow down to enjoy her company.
Angrily, she sweeps life's events in front of her broom
Like so many dust bunnies,
Anxious to get them out of the house.

It's only when she's with her grandchildren
That she relaxes.
She wears a serene smile,
Rocking slowly in her chair,
Letting the dust bunnies
Settle where they may,
While the children play at her feet,
As yet unaware
Of Grandmother's power.

LIFE
By Donald E. Sherwood

Only the hale can prevail
When overrun emotionally
By irrational people.

Sometimes frail succeed
When others cannot.

When details are ignored
By historians irrationally;
For twisted reasons.

Sometimes frail succeed
By efforts via solitude.

Because clan members
Underestimate those who
Are artesian by nature.

Surprises occur among those
Hale enough to plan ahead,
For life along a vale.

ONE AND DONE
By James Fly

The way we do anything
is the way we do everything,
but if we try to do everything,
we can do nothing.

So just do something;
do one thing--one
and anything becomes everything
done....

CHRISTMAS
By Donna Whittaker

C hrist's
H oliday for
R emembering
I mages of a
S hining star
T ilting toward
M ary and Joseph
A nd their
S pecial Son!

ANGELS SHARE
By James Fly

Angels share
because they care
not just for themselves
but also for others,
seeing everyone as sisters and brothers,
sharing a common humanity,
the bond of a one-blooded family.

"ANGELS SHARE" Photo by James Fly

PAPA'S LAP
By Jill Perkins

Tears running down my dirty cheeks,
I ran in the house to escape bullies in the street.
"Papa, Papa," I yelled as I burst through the door,
Crying out in pain, I crumbled to the floor.
My comfort began almost as soon
As my Papa's giant frame entered the room.
He bent and picked me up right there,
And gently carried me to his rocking chair.
Between gasping hard for big gulps of air,
I sobbed out my fears and all my cares.
He wiped my wounded knee with the sleeve of his shirt,
Then he proceeded to kiss away all of the hurt.
His fingertips softly brushed the dirt from my face,
And of the tears, left not even a trace.
Laying my head back upon his strong chest,
My troubled soul found peace and rest.
Ear pressed against his ribs, I felt sweet relief,
As I listened to the music of Papa's heartbeat.
So I can give to you this advice now:
When the evils of this life knock you down,
Spend some time just basking at your Father's feet.
You'll find all Satan's demons will retreat,
For His Word will light up your pathway,
When you crawl upon Papa's lap to pray.

MOTHERLY ADVICE
By Julie L. Casey

Listen my child; heed what I say.
If you plan to do something different today —
Something outrageous, crazy, or fun,
Adventurous, daring, second-to-none —
There's only one thing to ask, one thing to ponder,
One tenet to follow on that path that you wander:
This thing I plan to do,
Would my mother approve?

If the answer is yes, then proceed with full zest;
If the answer is no, you know not to go.
But if the answer be maybe and your resolve is torn,
Just think of who has known you since before you were
born.
Picture her face, her eyes, her smile,
Imagine her hands as she pauses for a while
To check your activity, to discover your choice;
Imagine her countenance, no need to hear her voice.
If her smile remains, better yet, broadens,
Be assured that your plans are undoubtedly good ones.
But if her smile disappears and her eyes become sad,
You'll know that the path you're following is bad.

I'm not telling you this to trick or control you,
Nor to stifle, confuse, embarrass, or annoy you.
There's only one reason I ask the above:
The best reason of all —
Your mother's love.

"JESSICA" Pencil drawing by Julie L. Casey

GOT TO BE GATSBY....
By James Fly

Behind the mask of respectability
lurks the demon of hostility,
his refined and polished manners
turn into fists like smashing hammers
when provoked by jealousy
he takes the insult personally,
he can't deflect it graciously,
leaving questions but no answers.
You can't repeat the past, it's said
and that's a given once you're dead--
Impeccably dressed in the coffin alone
with all the partygoers gone home,
the mansion's no more glamorous
and the mood anything but amorous,
"Old Sport" Nick's relationship onerous,
his life no longer his own.
He reached for her in his soul at night
across the bay toward the emerald light
Got to be the Great Jay Gatsby
and his obsessive love for Daisy
covered for her in the hit-and-run,
took the bullet from the husband's gun,
there's more to life than having fun,
bootlegger's cocktail for making crazy.

AUTUMN
By Betty Sill

I stand in awe at the splendor
Of the multi-colored trees.
It's such a pretty painted picture,
The leaves in the autumn breeze.

This beauty overtakes me;
I often catch my breath.
The artist painting pictures
For those who love Him best.

The hills are of every imaginable color;
The beauty more than I can behold.
Who is like unto Him,
Painting leaves orange, red, and gold?

BROADWAY RUN
By James Fly

I am the bullied and nerdy Peter Parker,
bitten by a bioengineered spider,
transformed into a human arachnid
masking my identity from my loyal girlfriend--
her name is Mary Jane Watson--
the beautiful redhead, the hottest one!
I weave my aerial web, a costumed vigilante
fighting techno villains
in a metropolitan Dante....

I am the New Amsterdam,
New York's oldest theatre,
restored after decades of neglect
and disrepair,
when the rats scurried through the mezzanine
and the rain soaked the seats
through a triple-X neon dream
until the 90's when Disney came along,
scored new Tin Pan Alley songs--
from the Lion King and Mary Poppins,
rubbing their magic lamp of Aladdin......

I am the boisterous Elder Cunningham
a renegade Latter Day Saint
from utopian Salt Lake--
on my mission to the profane Ugandans,
writing my very own version
of the Book of Mormon,
protecting the women from circumcision,
standing up to the warlord's intimidation.

And I am angel boy Moroni Elder Price
hiding behind a golden smile of nice,
in my starched white shirt
and narrow black tie
always asking the question of why
I can't live in Disneyland
under the spell of Tinkerbell's wand.....

I am the prince searching desperately
for the beautiful owner
of the one and only lost glass slipper,
and I am also Cinderella
riding in a crystal carriage,
looking for a prince's invitation to marriage,
longing for happily ever after
away from servitude
to my wicked stepmother....
but somehow, isn't it always something
how at the stroke of midnight
the carriage turns back into a pumpkin?
Where in the forest is the fairy godmother
at the darkest hour when you most need her?

I am Guy singin' and strummin'
my song of lost love
on the cobblestone streets
of contemporary Dublin,
meeting the Czech Girl,
feeling the attraction, needing her affection
while oblivious to the reality
of her situation:

separated from her husband, taking care of her
daughter,
providing a home for her friends and her mother;
Still, we make beautiful music together,
but we both know it simply can't last forever;
and when it comes time for me to go,
I surprise her with the piano,
bought with the money me dad gave me,
a bittersweet benediction
to the end of the show.......
Once we were one
and now two, twice--
why does fire have to freeze into ice?

You and I are the audience and we are the actors,
we are the producers and the choreographers,
and we're all in this drama workshopping together,
creating live and living theater,
by darkest night and brightest day
no matter what age,
on our very own Broadway stage.
Some of us are born to be divas and stars
and others understudies,
but we all have our roles to play,
none of us are nobodies.
And there's one thing that I've learned
on my lifelong Broadway run:
I can only turn the dark off
if my light is switched on........

"BROADWAY RUN" Photo by James Fly

BROKEN PIECES
By Betty Sill

Picking up the pieces
Of my broken heart.
So many tiny pieces,
I shouldn't even start.

Hate, fear, and anger
Burned out of control,
Dashing me to pieces,
Revealing my soul.

As I looked upon the scene,
I wondered if I could find
One willing or patient enough,
Or who would spend the time.

For my heart was very fragile,
If time could only mend
All the broken pieces
So it could beat again.

Picking up the fragments,
I come to understand.
Carefully, I placed them
In the safety of God's hand.

PUNCT*YOU*ATION
By James Fly

Our lives are punctuated
by the pauses of commas,
the finality of periods.
the hyphens of connection
the apostrophes of possession,
and the colons of emphasis.
But only a parenthesis
makes sense of the sentences......

Now
the past is past
it didn't last
and good or bad
we can't change it.
the future is future
it's not here yet
and light or dark,
we can't arrange it.
Now ignites the torch
that illuminates the present
now burns eternity's singular moment.....

Bleak Friday
the very day after
and now the day of
giving thanks for the things we need,
we storm the beachheads of corporate
and consumer greed.
Armed with plastic,
we seek bargains fantastic

for the latest digital gadgetry
and ultimate connectivity.
Forgetting in our frenzied plans
that only as we clasp our hands
together
around Thanksgiving's table
are we truly able
to relate authentically......

THE GREATEST ARTIST
By Susan Walter

His canvas is the whole wide world,
The brush, his mighty hand,
His palette made so beautifully,
He's the Teacher in command.
His clouds are white and billowy
With a hint of pink and gray.
He paints each slender blade of grass,
To make a perfect day.
The flowers are carefully tinted
In shades of red and blue;
The water added, so to match
The sky of azure hue.
Surely such a picture
Could only have been planned
And brought before our very eyes
By God's artistic hand!

FIRST KISS GOOD-BYE
By Jill Perkins

That cold autumn night stands so clear in my mind,
As if I just stepped backwards a lifetime.
We were just young adults, eager to come of age,
And in this new friendship, we'd just engaged.
Leaping from our hearts, the words we did share,
Were frosty clouds in the cold night air.
I hoped in my heart that this would never end,
As we cast our fates out on the cold night wind.
Then you turned to me with a lover's sigh,
And gave to me our first kiss good-bye.
'Twas but one kiss on a cold autumn night,
Beneath a harvest moon's golden light.
But I, so youthfully foolish, did believe,
'Twas a sign from above that I'd received.
You wandered in and out of my life over the years,
And you always brought with you heartaches and tears.
No matter how hard we might try,
You always ended up, kissing me good-bye.
There's nothing of that first love left today,
And we've long since gone our separate way.
But sometimes still, on a cold autumn night,
Under the magic of a harvest moon's light,
I swear, the wind carries on it a lover's sigh,
And the bittersweet memory of a first kiss good-bye.

"AUTUMN NIGHT" Photo by Julie L. Casey

HALF AND WHOLE
By James Fly

Two halves don't make a whole.
In fact, they dig the deepest hole
in any relationship,
turning intimacy into gamesmanship--
an unsatisfactory arrangement
and divisive estrangement.

You are whole within yourself;
you're not the better half of someone else
and they're not the part of you that's missing:
You are free to make your own decisions
in a kingdom where you reign as sovereign,
endowed with authority to lovingly govern.

But when two wholes meet each other
and decide as partners to join together
their bond becomes stronger
and their union lasts longer
than those who try to supply the lack:
the perception that they're only half......

HIS UNSEEN KISS
By The Holy Spirit through Jill Perkins

In the aching midst of
My life's most painful woe,
Feeling like a wretch
Cast down so low,
I was shown an act
Of such unconditional love.
It came as a miracle
Straight from Heaven above.
Around me comforting arms
Invisible, He lovingly slips.
And I softly felt the unseen
Kiss of Christ upon my lips.
I truly believe that
It did surely show;
My face must have been
A beautiful radiant glow.
For there was no doubt
I would never be the same,
Since Jesus kissed me
And whispered my name.

INAUGUR*ALL*
By James Fly

The landmark 13th Amendment
abolishing slavery
remains perhaps, Lincoln's enduring legacy,
a monumental act of personal bravery
in the face of hatred, prejudice
and the basest knavery.

It paved the way for the inauguration
of the first black president in a unified nation
who begins today his second term,
making some cheer and others squirm--
I pray he never comes to harm.

Martin Luther King Jr. could see the prize
he climbed the mountain and saw with his eyes
then he climbed back down and an assassin's bullet
took his life,
just as another one did to Abraham--
Ford's Theater-- eighteen hundred and sixty five..

But the dream would not die
would not be buried in the ground,
more than a century later, the lost would be found
and not only found, but elevated
elected, respected--
inaugurated
on the mall
for All.

LUNCH
By Betty Sill

Sitting at the table
Having lunch with Him,
Receiving bread and water
Never will I
Hunger or thirst again!

"LUNCH" Photo by Julie L. Casey

GOODNESS GREATNESS
By James Fly

Two wicked sister witches
and a good one named Glinda,
vying for power in a land of enchanted splendor,
intrigue at the palace of a murdered father
and the prophecy of another wizard
to rescue the jackbooted city of Emerald.

Prestidigitation!
the magical incantation
of the carnival magician--
heartthrob/breaker of women
chased by the strongman
transported to Oz by a rogue tornado,
meek and powerless, out of control,
the floating balloon of a bumbling buffoon,
yet protected in an iridescent bubble
when pursued by flying baboons
of vicious trouble....

Landing in a land
where good people are forbidden to kill,
but where wicked witches do it at will.
A romantic triangle,
a feeling of betrayal
confirmed by the image in the crystal ball,
the bite of a proffered poisoned apple,
electrifying fury, the jade of jealousy,
latent and subliminal.

Then a flight to the light of the dawning east,
from the cauldron of darkness in the desolate west,
a tornadic terrorist
toying with her non-wizard marionette
delivering a dire and ominous threat:
"You'll be the first one I put to death."

But even when the wizard didn't believe in himself,
Glinda believed and never gave up--
"If you believe, anything is possible,"
and if you believe in someone,
they become invincible.

A march on the city by straw soldier decoys,
"Dare they," said the witches, "march now on us?"
The Trojan horse of the stereoscopic wagon
and the con man and charlatan
becomes the illusionary sultan,
a parallel world Edison,
waiting patiently for Dorothy and Toto,
the cowardly lion, tin man and scarecrow.

Hypnotized at first by the glimmer and glitter,
the taker of treasure becomes a generous giver
of meaningful and lasting gifts:
a family for the China Doll,
and for the monkey, his friendship,
a thingamabob for the tinker
a smile for surly Snook
and his trumpet of fanfare....

And then he waved the wand of decree,
proclaiming the inhabitants to always be free...

he became a man with a righteous cause,
the Wonderful Wizard,
the Wizard of Oz.

We may not be exactly
what people have been looking for,
but we just may be the ones they need
to open the door
to walk the yellow brick road of the future,
and we and they can never say,
"He or she made me this way,
they did this to me,
we bear no responsibility."

We must use what we have,
the things we've packed in our own little bags;
there's always room to grow
and we're more capable than we know.

We may not be in Kansas any more,
but wherever we go, there we are,
till suddenly we become awake
and we no longer live our lives to be great
but strive instead for goodness,
the goodness inside, that's always been there
It's time to remember who we really are,
and not what we've become:

As homesick Dorothy eloquently said,
clicking her heels of ruby red,
"There's no place like home....
there's no place like home.......

And while others can help us get there,
we must ultimately go there
by ourselves--
alone.

BALANCING
By Donald E. Sherwood

Balancing efforts this winter so as
Not to be in line for a reverse yet.

Faltering some this evening as not
Able to confine thoughts to verse yet.

A thought is not an impulse until
Written down in verse.

Faltering some by snibbling words so
Not to confirm someone's fleece yet.

Coveting efforts by others by
Uttering not so divine words,
Can inverse good efforts:
Leading to a decline.

THE AFRICAN AMERICAN HABERDASHER
By James Fly

He walked with style and a certain verve,
he dressed above the sartorial curve,
an ambassador for designer hats and scarves--
the African American haberdasher
in his shop at Hallmark's exclusive Crown Center.

Proud owner of both Kangols and Stetsons,
an English derby was his prized possession.
"Try it on," he offered with singular intention
"and you, sir, will be a man of distinction."
He doffed his derby, looked me straight in the eye,
his eight-ball skull matched the cue ball of mine--
the African American haberdasher
in his shop at Hallmark's exclusive Crown Center.

"Even the gangstas in the twenties and thirties
wore hats and suits, nothin' torn or dirty--
why Al Capone wouldn't be shot dead
wearin' the saggy pants of rapper threads.
A man's not fully dressed till a hat's on his head,
that, my friend, is the standard of measure,"
he said in a voice as soft as calfskin leather.

For this sophisticated ebony gentleman
with features as fine as a polished mandolin
dress manifests the wardrobe within.
For him proper dress was a necessary pleasure
and his collection of hats his particular treasure,
the crown of his closet which without acquisition
would constitute a serious wardrobe malfunction.--

the African American haberdasher
in his shop at Hallmark's exclusive Crown Center.

"I only own four baseball caps but I rarely wear them,"
"Neither do I, so what are they for then?"
"They're for baseball games--
you wear a hat to fit the occasion--
a derby to church or maybe to shows equestrian."
He bemoaned the fact that modern dress
had rumpled into sloppiness.
Could he be related to Carroll's Mad Hatter?
Yet I had to admit he looked exceedingly dapper--
the African American haberdasher
in his shop at Hallmark's exclusive Crown Center.

We tipped our hats as I turned to go,
he winked slyly at me with a slight little bow,
"You gotta wear a hat to be the star of the show,
that's really the trademark of a man in the know."
said the African American haberdasher
in his shop at Hallmark's exclusive Crown Center.
I realized then what he was telling me,
why he emphasized especially
that a balding guy's head's not complete sans chapeau--
it's the masculine wig of the hairless male ego!

"MICHAEL MILLER", owner of *The Missing Piece*, Crown Center, Kansas City, Missouri
Photo by James Fly

EYES THAT SEE
By Betty Sill

Give me eyes to "see"
Like a blind man sees
Not just the surface,
But what's inside of humanity.
Help me to clearly see
The hurt, the pain, the agony;
Where the cold wind blew,
Marring their souls,
Leaving the desolate
Out in the cold.
Give me eyes that see
Beneath the garments they wear;
Give me a heart
That really does care.
Give me a word
Of comfort and cheer.
Help me to look
At what's really inside;
Don't let me sneer
Or turn them aside.
Give me a heart
Full of compassion,
Hands that are willing to work;
Give me the love,
For without it,
Christianity is not a flame,
Merely a flickering candle
Carried by saints hoping for fame.

A MOTHER'S PRAYER
By Patti Bennett

Dear Lord, each day
I feel eyes peering at me.
My blue-eyed girl follows
in my footsteps, going where
I go.
Lord, make me worthy
to lead her.
My son with eyes of brown
watches my hands,
doing what I do.
May I guide him in ways
pleasing to You.
May I be a responsible
example.
Lord, grant me
wisdom
and strength to lead them
close to you.
Thank you, Lord, for
the awesome
privilege of motherhood.

THE WEAKEST SPOKE
By James Fly

Lance finally admitted
he used drugs to win it,
not just once but seven times over,
a competitive conspiracy so undercover--
the recycling odyssey of a cancer survivor
and compulsive liar.
He opened up to Oprah
his first mea culpa.
After years of denial
and threat of a trial,
stripped of his medals
he continued the guile,
his laser beam eyes
betrayed the hint of a smile....
But overwhelming evidence
weakened resistance
until helmetless, the spokeless spokesman
finally admitted,
yes,
he used drugs to win it.
And as an enforcement
Nike cancelled his contract endorsement--
But they couldn't just do it
until they knew he did it.
The last will be first and the first will be last,
the future will come, erasing the past,

the pedals will stop their circular motion
and the roadside fans will cease their devotion,
the bicycle chains will oxidize to rust
and the phalanx of riders disintegrates to dust.
So, is there a moral to Armstrong's story?
It may well be life's cruelest joke--
cycling for trophies and podium glory
with an unconscious conscience
bends the weakest spoke....

ILLNESS

By Donna Whittaker

Dedicated to Sue Newham's memory (passed away June
1993)

Hope, fear
Quiet desperation
Uncertainty
Each new symptom
Brings more anxiety.

Positive thoughts,
Hope, optimism
Become harder
To feel and to think.

One day at a time
Sometimes.....
One hour at a time,
We get by.

We see fear in our
Family's eyes,
We try to maintain hope.
We search for answers.

Afraid to ask "why me?"
We pray for God's
Light, power, protection,
Presence and love.

What will tomorrow bring?
Only God knows!

We place our faith
In Him
And
We get by
A day at a time
An hour at a time
Hoping, praying!
Till we can say
"I'm much better!
Thank you!"

Thank the Lord!

PURA VIDA
By James Fly

Pura Vida--
the beautiful mantra of Costa Rica,
She waits like a mother for those who seek her,
fall on her lap, it's a place that's unique here....
where the weak grow strong
and the strong grow weaker....
She holds in her arms the world of the future
with army disarmed toward a culture of nurture
where the land is protected
and all beings respected.

Pura Vida--
Today I resolve to live a pure life
I can no longer handle personal scandal or strife.
I must be aligned with my authentic truth
to consistently live a life of true worth.
For me to be a positive influence
my head and my heart must join hands in congruence.
When I'm facing temptation, depression, elation--
to dissolve the illusion, resolve the confusion
at the core of my being where sightlessly seeing
I ask only one question that transcends obsession
to make reality real:
How does this person,
action, situation--
make me really feel?

"PURA VIDA" Photo by James Fly

MARROWTHON
By James Fly

A double explosion at the finish line,
the siren scream
and frightened stampede,
runners oblivious of place and time.
Limbs amputated,
families devastated,
victims of the Brothers Tsarnaev
never even knew what they died of;
that was left to the conscious survivors--
and the first responders when they arrived there.

Makeshift tourniquets
tied around bleeding stumps
a dancer's foot gone
and her valiant vow to dance on....
Adrianna's still singing her song
she's Boston strong.

Instant heroes,
Good Samaritan Jane and John Does
yet three dorm mates in spite of consequence,
conspired to conceal incriminating evidence
and what about Tamerlan's American wife, Catherine?
A recent convert to Islam,
was she a silent accessory assassin

or just another brainwashed victim
of her domineering husband?
Where was her attention
when the bombs were assembled in the kitchen?

Flags at half-mast,
casualties blessed—
Chechen Brothers,
jihadist bombers,
killing the infidel,
creating a living hell.
why do allahs demand violence of followers?
to smell the incense of sulfurous intolerance?

Dzhokhar's note scribbled in the boat
spoke to the motive the attack provoked:
the casualties were merely collateral damage
never mind the fact they were made in God's image.

A failure to assimilate
fertilized the seeds of hate.
Tamerlan said, "Those Americans,
I just don't understand them—
I claim none of them as my friends,
they bombed Iraq and Afghanistan,
we'll target the Boston Marathon!"
The amateur pugilist
could not win with his fists—
Downloading files of Al Qaeda's Inspire

lit the fuse,
ignited the fire.

The Russians warned the CIA,
who alerted the FBI,
but somehow both agencies,
struggling with conspiracies,
turned a blind and bureaucratic eye.

A city on lockdown,
the carjacking, gunfight and knockdown,
the hovering helicopter,
the sudden SWAT team capture,
the continuing investigation,
Bostonian celebration.

Back on Boylston Street,
empty now of runner's feet—
Three dead and thirteen amputees,
memorial display of bouquets and wreaths—
business not as usual,
life not as casual....

All eyes turn toward Boston,
with empathetic compassion
for we have lost with them.
We feel it in our deepest marrow,
dazed and confused,
incomprehensible sorrow,

facing our own uncertain tomorrow....

But random acts of senseless violence
fueled by hate can never silence
intentional ones of genuine kindness,
for love alone defuses
bombs of blindness,
clearing the way for us to break
the evolutionary tape
and finally cross the finish line
on our collective marathon.

A HERITAGE OF FAITH
By Mary Jane Fields

A few lapel pins showing Sunday School attendance
A box of yellowing envelopes and paper
A diary dated 1912,
An old trunk holds these things.
A faded, torn blue work shirt
A well worn Bible...
Not much of value in the eyes of the world,
The bankers, accountants and courts
(The 'big people' who count!)
But what of the other things....
The true legacy?
If the wind is in the right direction I can hear him
whistling
As he walks across the field behind our house...
Or hear his voice clearly from the choir loft of his little
church
Singing 'How Great Thou Art'.....
And meaning it!
The walnut trees he planted as three-inch sprigs
Now blow in the breeze, nodding their approval
Of his faith.
The birds that still return to the boxes he built
And the bushes he planned for their forefathers
Sing their thanksgiving
For his faith.
The leaves on the tall oaks he planted as twigs
Turn crimson in the fall, in celebration
Of his faith.
The house he built wears a new coat of paint
And rings with giggles of his own great grand child

On the floor he laid so many years ago,
In faith.
No old trunks or rooms of trunks could contain
The faith he had in his 80 plus years...
Faith in his present
Faith in the future
Faith in his family
Faith in his God...
He had enough for all
Because his faith lives on,
(Not in a rusting trunk or a pretentious bank vault)
But in the lives of all he touched,
In the soil he tilled
In the seeds he planted in the earth
And in the hearts of all he touched.
Therein lies his legacy to mankind
And to his heirs....
A fortune in memories
And faith.

THE KING
By Betty Sill

You may have seen the seven wonders
Descended beneath the earth,
And viewed magnificent scenes.
You may have climbed a mountain peak
And gazed at clear mountain streams.
But eyes have never seen,
Nor ears have ever heard
What is laid in store
For those who love His appearing.
No words can describe Him.
You may have gazed into the stars,
Used a telescope to view the galaxies.
Not a diamond or a jewel,
Nor a crown that ever sat
On the head of a king.
Nothing compares to His majesty;
He is the wonder of wonders,
A sight beyond our dreams.
Vocabularies are not adequate;
It is impossible to describe
The magnitude of His glory,
Or go to the extreme in any expression.
He is the wonder of wonders,
Christ Jesus, the King.
Although His birth was in a Bethlehem barnyard,
He is still a deity.
He grew up and associated
With common people.
He is touched by our pain;
A man of sorrows, he bore our grief.

He innocently died on a cross,
Our sins became His shame.
He was God's only son.
Multitudes and multitudes,
From every nation and all generations,
Hail Him, KING of all KINGS!

"JESUS" Pencil drawing by Julie L. (Powell) Casey

BROWN WORK GLOVES
By Patti Bennett

Yesterday,
    Dad wore brown work gloves
        to cultivate the garden,
        to trim rose bushes,
        to mow lush lawns,
        to hull black walnuts,
        to rake autumn leaves,
        to plant tulip bulbs,
        to lift heavy loads.

Then one day,
    The Great Gardener
        called him home.

Today,
    I value his example.
    I love the good earth.
    I cherish his helping hands.
    I wear brown gloves proudly.

SECTION II

Short Stories

DO UNTO OTHERS...
By Jan Powell

Down the long, dimly lit corridor the condemned's entourage advances. Leading this solemn group are two, large, white-jacketed, male attendants. Next, is a priest with his head bowed, muttering prayers. I am third, the reason for this stroll to eternity. Last, in this grotesque review, swaggers the supervising physician.

"Father, forgive her for she knew not what she did. It has been written, 'Do unto others as you would have them do unto you,'" the black-robed man prays aloud. As this saintly man turns his head toward me, I can see the tears glisten on his face. He hangs his head and I am possessed with feelings of empathy and remorse. We continue on to that single, ominous door ahead.

My thoughts are swirling like a drowning man caught in a cold and murky eddy. Voices from the trial ring in my ears like chanting demons needing to be exercised.

"She was such a good and compassionate nurse. Why, she was the top student in her class. If she pulled the "plug" on that man, then she did the right thing. Everyone who has ever worked with her knows she isn't capable of murder."

"It's not right for anyone to play God. Who's to say that a cure for a disease isn't just around the corner? We in the medical must preserve life no matter what the cost."

"This nurse has an impressive record of helping others. She is a wife and mother. Her children should not have to grow up without her nurturing and guidance."

"In an advanced society such as ours, we cannot allow mercy killers to go unpunished. So other murders of this type can be prevented, the prosecution demands the death penalty for the accused."

I look around me, trying to stop the voices pounding in my head by concentrating on the physical movements of those near me. Everyone seems to be moving in slow motion. It is as though I am a little girl again, taking those first, scary steps. But today, there is no loving parent to catch me if I fall. My captors are not smiling and will not prevent me from taking that final step toward the door of death.

Finally, we enter the forbidding room with its appropriate atmosphere for the doomed. It is a small, sterile dungeon, emitting cold drafts from every corner. In the center of the room waits a hospital examining table. Trays holding hypodermic needles and medicine vials are at one corner of the room. Small pipes jut out of the walls at carefully spaced intervals. A machine with the capacity of transmitting millions of electrical charges is positioned next to the deathbed.

As a large operating lamp is suddenly turned on, I find myself staring at the doctor. He has the look of a cold, calculating, machine. His eyes gleam with malice. There is an aura of pent-up excitement around him.

Long years of military discipline give him the appearance of one of the Gestapo hierarchy. In fact, he was chosen to be the director of this governmental department because of his past experiences in wartime executions. Over the years, he has experimented with Agent Orange, gas chambers, and other horrible ways of eliminating undesirables from our society. Our government has decorated him many times for his single-minded obsession. I count the medals on his lapel to keep from cringing from his touch. I am more frightened of this man than the possibility of impending death.

Silence hangs in the room like a heavy storm-laden cloud. The spell is broken when the doctor speaks. "Jane Doe, you have been convicted of euthanasia and sentenced to death by one of the following methods: high voltage electrical charges, gas inhalation, or injection of lethal drugs. An impartial computer will make the final decision. As the doctor in charge, I will only activate the machine. It alone will be responsible for your demise. Since this is the first computer execution, you will be remembered---not for your crime, but for the way you are put to death."

I am led to the cold, hard slab of steel and told to lie down. Why do I have this feeling of nakedness and exposure even though I am fully dressed? Sweat appears on my forehead and at my armpits. My bladder is full. I become nauseous and lightheaded. "Let me blackout and know no more," I pray to no avail.

"Do you want your eyes covered?" I am asked. My head nods yes, for I am terrified that at any moment I will lose my composure. Large, impersonal hands begin hooking wires to my head, arms, legs, and chest. A needle penetrates the skin of my arm in preparation for the inducement of drugs. Restraints are put on my wrists and ankles, rendering them helpless.

As I lay waiting for the final act to begin, I remember what terrible crime was committed. The patient's history: age 90, no family or friends, terminal cancer, not even a chance of survival. Day after day, he begged the nurses to allow the black angel of death to claim him. Finally, his plea to end his suffering was heeded.

Now that angel of mercy will surrender her life for that one moment of compassion.

One by one, they leave the room until I am alone, shaking with fear and dread. The doctor speaks over an intercom, breaking the eerie silence. "All is in readiness. We will begin."

I hold my breath to keep from screaming. "Please, God, let it end quickly," I implore. Time stands still as my deeds—good and bad—pass before my eyes. Why do only the good deeds keep appearing over and over?

I see a skinny little girl, with long mousy brown pigtails dangling down her back. She sits by the doll bed muttering kind, soothing phrases to her "patient" hoping to make her feel better.

For as long as she can remember, she has wanted to be a nurse when she grows up. Every doll and stuffed animal she owns is treated with doses of Kool-Aid and M & M's to ward off the evils of sickness. None of her patients die because she lives in a fantasy world.

As the vision of the little girl fades, I see an older version of the same girl. Only now, she is a teenager packing to go off to Nursing School. She is smiling and is very happy to be able to fulfill her childhood dream. Ahead lies four years of difficulties and hardships, but it will be worth it. Marriage and children will have to wait until her career is established.

Last to appear is the mature registered nurse. For five years she has been the Head Nurse on the busiest floor of the city's largest hospital. She looks so confident and professional in her white uniform and spotless orthopedic shoes. Other nurses are always teasing her about the halo above her head. Patients are charmed by her caring, dedicated service to their every need. When it comes to those under her care, she works tirelessly and relentlessly to make them well.

Her one desire in life is to end suffering for her charges. She believes in the quality of life as apposed to life's quantity.

Round and round these images spin before my eyes. I am on the edge of hysteria when a voice with heavenly appeal fills the room.

"The attendants will be in to help you off the table. Thank you for submitting to this trial run for tomorrow's computer execution. The experiment has been successful. See you all in the morning for the real thing," announces the jubilant doctor.

I am exhausted, limp, disoriented. I babble incoherently to myself. No longer am I the disciplined, self-assured medical assistant. The words of the priest ring through my head: "Do unto others as you would have them do unto you." I vow to no longer take part in executions for today I have been the other person.

May God have mercy on us all.

THE MEMOIRS OF MISS EMILY
By Susan Walter

Finally, I saw light and sunshine! It was dark and lonesome in the old box I was packed away in for almost 60 years. As I looked around me, I saw strange looking furniture, unlike the furnishings I was accustomed seeing in the parlor where I lived in Corning, Missouri. I guess those furnishings would be called antiques today.

After much deliberation, I decided to write my memoirs. Surely, there would be interesting facts I could write about before I was packed away in that dreadful old box again. I am an unusual author. You see, I AM A DOLL.

"What can I write about?" I thought to myself as I looked around for a quill pen. That's odd, the pen I found did not look like a quill pen at all, but it works. As nearly as anyone can figure out, I am 137 years old. Miss Alice, a member of the Walter family, received me as a gift when she was 5 years of age. I became Miss Alice's best friend around 1868. I don't know if I have any doll kinfolk.

My head, hands and feet are made of china. My body is cloth, stuffed with sawdust. The sawdust is so heavy, I tire carrying my body around. My hair is painted black. My cheeks are rosy pink and said to be dazzling against my white, shiny complexion. I have only one foot and I am saddened by it. I don't recall how my foot got broken off. My clothing is made of 100 percent cotton fabric purchased from the Walter Mercantile Store in Corning, Missouri and sewn by the nimble fingers of Miss Alice's mother, Mary.

Miss Alice was very good to me. She spent many

years cradling me in her arms. She rocked me into a slumbering state many times in her handmade rocker with a woven seat. Spring and summer were favorite seasons for me. In the early spring, the crocuses and daffodils would pop through the once-frozen sod. The blue morning glories showed off their ensembles as they entwined around the old trellis. When the hollyhocks bloomed, Miss Alice would pluck one of the blossoms, turn it upside down and it resembled a skirt. She used a tiny ball for a head; twigs would become the arms and legs. Presto! She had a doll.

One summer day, Miss Alice took me with her to pick raspberries. She found so many berries, she laid me on the plush green grass so she could use both hands. She was so excited about her find, she rushed home to show her mother. Oops! She forgot to pick me up!

"Miss Alice," I cried. "How could you forget me?" I listened for her footsteps, but heard only the rippling melodies of the birds. The coolness of the night would soon descend upon me. All of a sudden I heard a scrambling sound. "It's Miss Alice!" I squealed. "I knew you would come back for me." But, it wasn't Miss Alice. The noise was made by several mice running over the grass and sticks. One of them darted over my sawdust leg while another nibbled at my slick, shiny nose. If my hair had not been painted on, it would have stood up on end! I lay on the cool grass all night. The next morning, the dew was scattered over the grass like a broken diamond necklace. "Where are you, Miss Alice?" I cried out again. "Please, don't leave me here forever." Just as my hopes were fading, Miss Alice finally found me.

"Oh, Miss Emily, I'm so sorry. I didn't remember where I laid you," she cried as she hugged me. When I felt her little arms around me and lovingly squeezing me, everything was all right.

One day when the sunlight was streaming through the old walnut trees, Miss Alice took me on my first picnic. The sky soon turned to a grey-green, unlike the beautiful blue sky with floating whipped-cream clouds we saw when we left home. There was a rumble of thunder. The jagged forks of lightning frightened me. The wind began whistling through the huge walnut trees as the branches swayed. The rain began bouncing off the dry ground. "Miss Emily, you're getting all wet," Miss Alice sobbed as she protected me from the rain with the skirt of her dress. How nice it was to get home again.

One warm, sunny day, Miss Alice took me out play. "Alice, don't go near the goose pen," called her mother as she pumped a pail of water from the old well beside the house. "Those geese are mean. They might hurt you."

"I won't, Mama," Miss Alice called back. But, defying her mother's orders, Miss Alice held me tight as she headed straight for the goose pen. She stood on tiptoes to unlatch the gate. Immediately, we heard the language of the geese as they honked their way around us. They kept trying to peck at Miss Alice's legs as they darted from one side to another. "Mama, Mama, come get me!"

"Didn't I tell you not to go near that pen?" questioned her mother. "I love you and I don't want you to get hurt. Go inside the house and think about what you have done," her mother instructed as she pulled me away from Miss Alice.

Miss Alice had many tea parties. I was always her special guest. She served make-believe tea in beautiful cups. Many of her dishes came from England. Folks around Corning considered Miss Alice's parents wealthy, whatever that means.

As the years passed, Miss Alice grew to be a lovely woman. I was packed away and put in the Walter attic. When the lid closed, I mumbled to myself, "Oh, my, how long will I be in here?"

Miss Alice died in 1934 at the age of 71. She never married. I heard she had a boyfriend, but her daddy didn't like him. Many years passed. From the Walter attic, I was taken to a family member's home in New York. I remained in that home, still packed away, for many years. In August 1995, I journeyed with this family to St. Joseph, Missouri, where I was unpacked from the yellowed pages of the newspapers, dated 1878. What a relief! My new owner stripped me of my stained, yellowed dress, petticoat and pantalets. She laundered them.

"You sure are a mess," my new owner, Susan, said. "I'm taking you to the Doll Hospital. Perhaps the doctor can keep you from falling apart."

"She has a beautiful face," the lady doctor commented. I was happy to hear that. "I'll tighten her arms, repair her body, and try to find her another foot." Another foot! I'll have two feet again. My sawdust heart jumped with joy. I remained at the hospital for two weeks. I mended nicely, but the doctor could not find me another foot.

I don't know what will happen to me now. I hope I can stay with Susan forever. She will probably prop me up on her bed to show me off to her friends and say, "Hasn't she aged nicely?"

"CHINA DOLL" Photo by Julie L. Casey

SANTA'S STOCKINGS
By Betty Sill

Santa was nestled and snuggled in bed; with a pillow, he covered the back of his head. Mrs. Claus called, "It's time to get up." The coffee was steaming all black and hot; in the cold winter weather, Santa would need a full pot. The aroma in the kitchen was spicy and sweet. Santa would be hungry for something to eat.

Mrs. Claus listened to hear the creak of the boards in the floor, as always it did creak under Santa's chubby little bare feet. But not a creak did she hear, not even a sound. She walked quietly down the hall; slightly she opened the door, and looked in with a peek. Santa lay there, deep in sleep. She tiptoed in, amused by the sound of his snore; gently she shook him, but she spoke not a word.

Santa groaned, rolled over, then leaped out of bed. "Sweet dreams were swirling all around in my head," he said with a smile that looked like a smirk.

Mrs. Claus handed Santa his thermal underwear. "Put these on," she said, looking through her glasses. She gave him a glare. Santa got dressed, just like she said. He put on his thermals and his red Santa suit; a red stocking cap covered the top of his round, bald head.

He looked for his stockings — he owned quite a few — but not a one could be found. He called Mrs. Claus, who had some explaining to do.

"I couldn't resist, in spite of myself; I filled your stockings for the homeless, the needy, and those who live alone," she said, her face shining with glee.

Santa Claus stood there with tears in his eyes. He spoke with a nod of his head. "These stockings will make a wonderful surprise."

Santa's heart was beating with joy and delight as he piled those stockings high on top of the sled. Climbing aboard to the seat of his sled, he tuned to his wife and, politely, he said, "Merry Christmas, Mrs. Claus. You are a jolly little elf, thinking of others and not just yourself."

THE LADY OF THE NIGHT
By Jan Powell

She was born to become a lady of the night. Her hair was long and black with a silky shine. When she walked, her bottom would sway back and forth with a provocative swish. To keep her protector happy, she did her best work at night.

In the wee hours of the morning, she would stand on the corner of a street to enhance the best possibilities to lure the prey. Because she was small and willowy, she was at a disadvantage. But her nails were long and sharp and she could fend off any competitor with ease.

The corner was mostly deserted, but still there was a lot of activity. She only chose the best specimens that the location could offer. She always appeared in a black coat summer or winter. The prey was always surprised by the speed of her movements, the perkiness of her ears to hear everything around her.

As the years passed, she became less and less able to attract the rewards her protector demanded of her. She walked slower, her coat was wearing thin; she lacked her swagger she once had. It was time to retire from her profession. The streets at night no longer appealed to her.

On her last night of work, she brought home a big hairy looking male and dropped it at his feet. She cuddled up to her best friend; he promised to take care of her the rest of her life. He told her that she was indeed the best lady of the night he ever had.

She quite loudly purred her content as they admired the rat.

"LADY OF THE NIGHT" Pencil drawing by Julie L. Casey

A SHORT STORY
By Charles Gilliland

It was a slow day at the screen-printing shop that Rick Vernon owned in Derby, Kansas, so he decided to close early and set up a tee time at a golf course in nearby Wichita. Upon arriving home, he checked his answering machine and found a message from Laura Corbet, his former high school sweetheart. She wanted Rick to call her as soon as he got the message.

Laura and Rick had started going steady during their freshman year and things quickly grew serious between the two. They surely would've married after they graduated from high school, but things became sour for the Corbett family the summer before Rick and Laura's junior year when the steel plant where Laura's dad worked shut down, leaving him with no job.

Unable to find other work and his employment benefits running out, the family had no choice but to accept a job offer from a relative in Brookings, Oregon on a fishing boat that he owned. Although the work would be seasonal and risky, the pay would be good, so the Corbet decided that it would be their best, and only, option to pull up stakes and move to Oregon.

Laura and Rick stayed in touch over the five years she had been living in Oregon, mostly by cards and letters. So he was surprised to get a phone call from her; what Laura wanted to tell him must be really important for her to be willing to incur long distance charges. Golf game forgotten for the moment, Rick dialed the number she had left on the recording machine.

When she answered, Rick identified himself and told Laura that he got her message. She told Rick that she was glad he called her back and they engaged in idle chitchat for a few minutes. Then she told him the reason she wanted to talk to him. Laura had decided that she wanted to move back to Derby; she missed the area and everyone she knew. It seemed like it was always raining in Oregon and, to add insult to injury, the roof on the house Laura was renting had started leaking. Since the landlady was turning a deaf ear to her complaints, Laura was getting ready to move out. She had started selling everything she had that wouldn't fit in a suitcase, with one exception — Laura had recently took a liking to and bought a fully restored 1967 Chevrolet Impala. Rick remembered some photos that Laura had sent of her with the car in a previous letter.

Laura had looked as appealing to him as she always had, and the Impala had looked great as well. It was a bright yellow with a black interior and had been fitted with custom wheels made of aluminum. Laura was going to keep the car and, rather than try to drive to Kansas in a twenty-odd-year-old vehicle, she was going to have it shipped by truck and fly to Wichita, picking up the Impala when it arrived.

She told Rick that it would be three weeks when her flight would land at the airport in Wichita and was wanting to know if Rick could pick her up at the airport, then later help her collect her car when it arrived.

Rick told Laura, with much enthusiasm, that he'd be more than happy to do so. With that settled, Laura told Rick the day and time her flight would arrive and when the car was supposed to be in the area.

After they'd finished their conversation and hung up, Rick decided to forget about playing golf that evening. He and Laura had talked for over an hour and the prospect of his old flame moving back into town had him too excited to think about anything else.

Instead, Rick spent the rest of the evening and most of the night recalling the times they'd had together and her silky, shoulder-length hair, her figure that was a little stocky, but in all the right places, and how he just couldn't wait for the day when Laura's plane would land.

The excitement was short lived, however, when a week and a half later the Pacific Coast was hit by the worst storm in many years, with the Brookings area being among the hardest hit.

Rick had been following the news story closely, keeping tabs on the destruction, all power and communications having been cut off in the area. There had been a number of people injured, killed, and missing. Many of the missing were thought to have been swept off Highway 101, which was built on the Oregon and California coastlines, when they were trying to either get home or flee to safety.

Rick tried to call Laura's home and sporting goods store where Laura worked without any success; the phones were still down. When service was finally restored, he succeeded in reaching a coworker who told Rick that Laura was among the missing. She wrote down Rick's name and phone number so that if she found out anything, she'd call him. He thanked her and hung up, then tried to resume his normal routine.

A week after his conversation with the sporting goods store worker, Rick was watching the Ten O'clock News when the report was aired that the last of the missing persons from the Pacific Coast storm was found. Divers had found a submerged car about 200 yards out in the sea where it had been swept off the coastal highway. The sole occupant of the vehicle was only described as an unidentified female in her early – mid twenties.

While the anchorperson was speaking off camera, footage showed a badly battered auto being pulled ashore by a tow truck. Rick's heart sank and tears welled up in his eyes when he saw the car being winched from the Pacific was a yellow 1967 Impala with aluminum custom wheels.

THE RING
By Jeannetta R. Danford

Two sisters were competitive to the point of jealousy. Nellie was tall and blond, typical of a first-generation American daughter of Swedish immigrants. Jennie tipped five feet by a couple of inches and had brown hair like their mother, though, to her regret, not nearly as thick and lustrous. Their two handsome, six-foot tall half-brothers worked hard on the family farm, but volunteered for the Navy as soon as the United States entered World War I. Jennie, as the youngest, worked as hard as the rest, her size not a consideration in what was expected of her, but had been allowed to continue in school through all the ten grades then available. At her graduation, her father was furious to see on her diploma that she had selected Margaret as a middle name instead of being just plain, sensible Jennie Anderson.

Swedish girls were in demand as household help in the town homes as they were diligent workers. With her brothers off to war, Mommy and Nellie could manage at home so, while still a teenager, Jennie soon located happily with the Granville family in one of the big houses in downtown Maryville. She worked temporarily with another family, but had to assist with cleaning and laundry as well as doing all the cooking. "I didn't stay long there! That woman didn't want to give me even a half day off and treated me like a servant." At the Granville's, she had a nice room of her own and could invite her girlfriends to visit her there. Her young man could call for her at the front door, too. Mrs. Granville often accompanied Mr. Granville on his buying trips for their local department store. On their return, Jennie always received a gift, as their family members did. Once they brought each of the females a peach satin chemise. "The latest thing!" they were informed.

The cooking was her entire responsibility with the exception of keeping the front porch swept and dusted, and the pillows fluffed on the wicker furniture. That was fun in the freshness of a lilac-scented dawn, and she didn't mind carrying lemonade glasses to the kitchen, dumping cigars and cigarettes, and wiping out the ashtrays. Mrs. Granville entertained frequently, and Jennie prepared fancy sandwiches and tall angel food cakes for the card clubs, mission groups, and other afternoon teas. "Near the Fourth of July, we put tiny flags on the little teacakes." Mrs. Granville was generous with her praise of Jennie's cooking and Jennie's friends, in similar situations, wished their employers were as kind.

Her time was her own after supper was over and the dining room and kitchen restored to order. She could meet friends downtown for a picture show, skating, or a root beer at Reynold's Drug Store. Evenings often ended with a rambling walk to the teachers' college, the three-story brick building at the edge of town.

Jennie was independent and in no hurry to get married. Her mother and Nellie stopped to see her if she wasn't too busy whenever they were in town. Her job was pleasant and her employers respected her. Her first love had impulsively married another girl while she and a girlfriend had gone to El Dorado, Kansas to help her uncle for a few months after high school. Of her boyfriend, she just shook her head and said mysteriously, "He did the right thing." The ruby friendship ring he had given her was a keepsake the rest of her life.

When another young man returned from WWI service in the Navy, they began seeing each other. He was eight years older, on his own after his mother remarried when he was fourteen, and not a good prospect, her parents thought. Not only that, he was slight of build and inches shorter than the men in her family. To Jennie, the criticism was like waving a red flag in front of a bull. Besides, Nellie had recently received a beautiful ring set with opals from a young farmer, and they were planning their wedding. Jennie was jealous.

Their dating was sporadic for several years but as Thad's evening visits increased to twice a week, Mrs. Granville talked to Jennie in a motherly fashion about his intentions. Jennie wouldn't admit that the courtship was becoming serious. She eventually gave in to his demands for an engagement, though informing him resolutely that she did not want an opal ring. She wanted no comparisons made between her ring and the one Nellie wore so proudly.

When Thad came to the door on a warm spring Saturday evening, he sniffed appreciatively. "Fried chicken and wilted lettuce?" She nodded, wishing there was some left to feed him. He was always so thin! They strolled the familiar brick pathway to the college grounds, Thad talking excitedly and walking almost faster than she could keep up. She knew something was going to happen. They selected a familiar spot under a large oak tree and he cleared a spot of freshly mowed grass for her to sit. Proudly, he presented the small grey box, which held her engagement ring. She looked at it. She looked at him. Set with opals, pretty enough, but hadn't he listened when she said she did not want an opal ring? "But everybody's wearing them," he stated, tight-lipped. "The jeweler said this is what every girl wants."

"Not this one," Jennie said sadly, and got up, brushed grass from her skirt, and walked back to the house. Alone.

Thad also rose, looking after her helplessly and angrily. He started his long walk back to the farm where he was working for the summer. His way home led him across the 102 River. On the bridge, he paused, took the ring from his breast pocket, admired it for a moment, then tossed it over the side. "That's the last engagement ring she'll get from me," he muttered, slightly appalled at what he had done.

It was weeks before Thad walked into town again and showed up on the Granville's front porch. When Mrs. Granville hesitantly called Jennie down from her room, she was glad to see him. The walks and simple amusements were resumed, but there was never any conversation about an engagement ring.

One Saturday evening, Thad announced that his government pay had come, for a small service-related disability, and he had rented an apartment in downtown Maryville and purchased furniture to fill it. Jennie was impressed. This would show her parents that Thad was amounting to something. And Nellie would be green with envy. Even so, the couple was cautious about making wedding plans. One late August day, on Jennie's afternoon off, they boarded the train and eloped to Bedford, Iowa, where they were married by a Justice of the Peace. They exchanged simple gold wedding rings and Jennie never wore another. The marriage remained a secret until she could tell her parents and she remained at the Granville's until they could reluctantly replace her. Thad stayed in the apartment alone. If either of them regretted the discarded opal engagement ring, it was never mentioned when they were together. The story is a part of family history, however, and is occasionally retold to illustrate either her stubbornness (his version) or his temper (her version).

CRUMPLED MEMORIES
Excerpt from Time Lost, a novel by Julie L. Casey

Time had always played a minor role in my life, lurking in the shadows and only bursting out to assert its pompous self-importance in the excruciatingly slow last three minutes of history class or the gut-wrenching last thirty seconds of our football game, when the other team had the ball and the chance to eek out the win. On other occasions, it would sweep events in front of it, in a hurry to get them over with and out of the way, like during our all-too-brief lunch periods or gone-in-a-flash summer vacations. But mostly, Time was something I never thought about; it was just another ever-present force like the geomagnetic field surrounding the earth. Who could know that both those constant, universal forces could be brought to their knees in a matter of seconds by a force greater than both of them?

I can barely remember when Time worked to my advantage, when it embraced me in its comforting arms and held my hand during long stretches of happiness. I remember walking to the park every day with my mother, one hand held securely by her, the other holding onto the snack she always brought me when she picked me up from daycare after work. We'd walk slowly to the swings, while Mom would ask me about my day and laugh at the cute little things I'd say. Then we'd swing together, mom on the next swing over, her hand covering mine while I grasped the chain of my swing. She'd help me swing that way, unlike the other moms, who pushed their kids from behind. I remember thinking that she was the coolest and most beautiful mom in the world. I have one particular picture of her in my mind: she is leaning back in the swing, her golden hair flowing out behind her; her eyes are closed and her mouth is curved into a big smile. I'm not sure if this is a real memory of her or one I've created to cope with the loss of that happy time.

Another snapshot I guard protectively, locked away in the chest of treasured memories in my mind, is of her opening the present I gave her that last Christmas before the split. I remember my dad taking a rare break from his endless pursuit of financial success to help me find the perfect gift for her, one that I was sure would ease the tension that I could feel growing in our household. I had an idea of what I wanted to get for her. Mom was a nurse at a family clinic just a few blocks from our house in North Kansas City. She always wore a nurse's watch pin on her sweater to use when she counted how many times a patient's heart would beat in one minute. Mom always wore a sweater over her scrubs; she was always cold, even in the summer, when she complained that the air conditioners made her feel like she was in the arctic. A few weeks before Christmas that year, her watch fob broke and she had had to carry the watch in her pocket instead of pinned to her sweater. In my still-childish, 12-year-old mind, I thought the broken watch was the source of her sadness and somehow the reason she was suddenly less available to me in the evenings, often leaving me at home alone until after dinner. Sometimes Dad would even get home before she did and I could tell it upset him that she wasn't there.

Dad took me to countless jewelry stores that Saturday before Christmas, until I finally found the perfect one: the watch face was set in a gold, heart-shaped case and suspended by a gold chain from a red, enameled bow, which had a pin on the back. As with all nurses' watch pins, the clock face was upside down so that Mom could see the second hand whizzing around while she took a patient's pulse. It was expensive — I remember Dad pulling out three hundred-dollar-bills to pay for it while he half-joked that just because my name was Benjamin didn't mean I should spend all his "Benjamins." It was the most I'd ever seen him spend on anything; I think he felt the importance of the gift, too.

On Christmas, Mom sat off by herself with a little sad smile on her face, watching me as I excitedly opened my new Xbox 360 and several games to go with it. Then I gave her my gift. The jewelry store had wrapped the gold box with a big red bow and I had made a little card shaped like a heart with a picture of us swinging drawn on it. Mom's eyes got all teary when she saw the card and when she opened the box, she merely smiled and held it against her chest, murmuring, "Thank you, my sweet boy." It wasn't the reaction I'd hoped for. I had envisioned her exclaiming with joy and embracing Dad and me in a giant hug, but she just sat there, trying not to cry. I remember being so confused and disappointed by her reaction and when I looked at Dad, he just looked sad. I think that is when I knew our family wouldn't be together much longer. I don't know how I knew; I just did. I grew up faster that day than in all the twelve years preceding it.

After the holiday break, I was almost happy to be back at school. I was already tired of playing video games by myself all day. Sometimes, one of my friends' moms would come pick me up and take me over to their house to spend the day, but since no kids my age lived in my neighborhood, I spent most of the holidays at home alone. Back at school, at least I had people to talk to for a good chunk of the day, which was a relief, even if I had to do some homework along the way. On the bus rides home from school, though, the loneliness would begin to swell up in my chest again, especially when we passed the park filled with happy toddlers and doting mothers. Even though I was way too old to swing and hold my mom's hand, I remember thinking that I'd give away everything I owned just to be able to spend another day with her in the park, while Time looked the other way and let us be for a while.

Time was no longer good to me; when I was alone, it crept along like a slowly melting icicle, but on the rare occasions that my parents would spend time with me, always separately and seeming desperate to win my favor, Time would flow like a raging river after the spring thaw. One bright, cold day in February, Dad moved to an apartment in the heart of Kansas City, just a few blocks from where he worked as an accountant on the 14th floor of the tallest building in Kansas City. I remember counting the floors of that building one day and discovering that it was really the 13th floor, but Dad explained that superstition about the number 13 made them skip it in tall buildings.

One unexpected benefit of Dad moving out was that he made a point of picking me up every weekend and actually doing things with me like playing video games and taking me out to eat. We got closer than anytime I could remember in my life, but at the expense of getting further away from Mom. Their divorce was final the summer after my 13th birthday, which is on April 13th, and I began to believe in the evil of that number. It seemed that being born on the 13th had destined me to an unlucky life. Mom seemed happier than she'd been in a long time and, for some reason, that angered me. When I found out that she had been dating one of the doctors at her clinic, I was furious — how could she betray both Dad and me, choosing someone else over us. I began to beg Dad to let me move in with him and before the next school year started, he agreed to ask Mom. She was adamantly opposed to the idea at first; I thought it was because she didn't want to look like a bad mother. I picked fights with her many times over stupid little things and at other times I was just angry and sullen. Finally, she reluctantly agreed, as long as Dad could arrange to drop me off and pick me up from my same school.

After I moved in with Dad, I began to see less and less of Mom. I just couldn't get over the fact that she was to blame for the breakup of our family. Even our phone conversations became strained and I began to ignore her calls when I saw her name on the caller ID. Once, when I was staying at her house on the weekend, she had her new boyfriend over to meet me and have dinner with us. I could barely be civil. If Mom deserved the blame for turning my world upside down, then this man had to be the reason she did it; he had to be more important to her than me. I was filled with anger and loathing toward him and it was all I could do to get through dinner without choking on the baseball-sized lump in my throat. I didn't see much of my Mom after that night. I made up excuses like I was staying at a friend's house or I didn't feel good, to avoid my weekends with her. I figured she'd rather spend the time with her new man anyway.

Mom and Lyle got married just before my 14th birthday, completing the misery of that unlucky year. I was forced to walk Mom down the aisle since her dad had died before I was born. I refused to say anything, though, when the minister asked, "Who gives this woman to be married to this man?" I just let her go and went to sit down, with my eyes on the floor for the rest of the ceremony. I didn't want to add a picture of this travesty to the treasure chest of memories in my head. After the wedding, Mom moved into a nice new house with Lyle and sold our family home. Now my childhood was boxed up and stored away like the memories of my happier days.

"CRUSH" Pencil drawing by Julie L. (Powell Halter) Casey

SECTION III

Essays

&

Memoirs

THE DEPRESSION
By Gloria Williams

Imagine—we survived the depression! It wasn't easy, but we didn't know how bad it was 'til later. We were all poor together.

We had muddy roads and it seemed my lot to push. I rarely got to church without mud all over my shoes or feet! We never seemed to have much money either. We kept a running bill at the mercantile and at harvest time we hoped to have good enough crops to cover it. We shared butchering with our neighbors and helped each other.

For Sunday I had one good dress. I wore it too big 'til it was too small. It was wine taffeta and I grew to hate it. I had overalls and some feed sack dresses. I had two pair of shoes and we wore them until they were completely worn out.

We had no electricity until I w as 16. We had no running water, only a weekly bath in the kitchen in a washtub. The bedrooms were cold and we had a gas stove in the dining room. The snow blew through the windowsill onto my bed. When it was summer time, we were as hot as we had been cold in the wintertime. We canned our garden stuff with no fans.

But we had family, friends, church, and good times together. We had parties and played games. We made paper dolls out of Sears catalogs, and had dollhouses made out of cardboard, and wallpaper books. We rode our bikes through mud puddles, or got up a baseball team. We roller-skated a lot and my knees were always scabbed over.

THE UNCERTAINTIES OF A CHRONIC ILLNESS
By Donna Whittaker

Tomorrow, will I be able to walk?
Tomorrow, will I be able to talk?
Tomorrow, will I be able to hold my head upright?
Tomorrow, will I be able to chew my food?
Tomorrow, will I be able to swallow my food?
Tomorrow, will I be able to breathe?

I can do all these things today because my myasthenia gravis (MG) is controlled with the medications I take. Myasthenia gravis is a chronic neuromuscular condition with various symptoms. The medications I take only last from one dose to the next dose, approximately four hours.

Tomorrow, will I be able to hold my eyes open?

Tomorrow, will double vision prevent me from driving?

Some patients only have ocular myasthenia gravis. Tape or eye crutches may be needed to hold their eyes open so they can see. Or, they may have double vision, which hindered my driving the summer my daughter was fifteen. I've always been an avid reader, but I may need to depend on books on tape like other MG patients.

Tomorrow, will I be able to climb stairs or enter my front door with its two steps?

Tomorrow, will I be able to raise my arms to brush my hair or brush my teeth?

My myasthenia gravis is the generalized juvenile autoimmune type. The neuromuscular junctions throughout my body often fail to operate properly. I've seen days when I couldn't walk in and out of the front door of my ranch-style home. At the same time, I could not raise my arms to brush my hair and my teeth so it was just as well that I couldn't go out in public looking unkempt. However, at that time it was frustrating to be unable to go to the laundry room in the basement to wash my baby's clothes.

Tomorrow, will I be able to hold the telephone receiver to my ear?

Tomorrow, will I be able to enunciate clearly to talk on the telephone?

Relatives called daily to see if I had had my baby, but I could not hold the receiver to my ear to talk to them. Or will my voice return to the stage where telemarketers hung up on me! They could not understand a word I said.

Who am I?

I am a wife, mother, daughter living in Middle America.

I have worked as a work-study student, a salesperson, a teacher, an insurance claims representative, a demonstrator, a regional manager, an assistant education director, and an adjunct college professor.

I have volunteered for Girl Scouts, Kansas City Myasthenia Gravis Association, MGnet, Myasthenia Gravis Foundation of America, Heartland Regional Medical Center, St. Joeys Clown Alley, Prodigy Online Service, "No More Stares" Conference, MERIL, American Heart Association, American Cancer Association, Muscular Dystrophy Association, St. Joseph Writers Guild and more.

Why may I be unable to do the above activities tomorrow?

Because myasthenia gravis has its ups and downs and no one can predict when symptoms will worsen or will subside. I am thankful for each day I can be active and relatively symptom free and pray that the medications will always be available that keep me productive.

Note: For more information about myasthenia gravis, see www.myasthenia.org or www.mgakc.org.

WEDDING MISHAPS IN OUR FAMILY
By Gloria Williams

At our wedding, we waited and waited for a bridesmaid to show up. When she finally arrived, we asked her, "What happened?" She replied, "I got in the car and on the way discovered I had lost one of my heels, so we rushed back and looked everywhere, but could not find it". So she went through the whole ceremony with one heel without a wobble.

At our son Gary's wedding, they brought our gorgeous tea roses and pinned them on us. We were all in the restroom checking our hose and hair, when the bride's mother leaned over and "kersplash," her bouquet fell into the toilet. We grabbed it out and rinsed it off. But we got the giggles, laughingly calling it her "PEE ROSE"

At this same wedding, we rushed to get everyone dressed and out the door. At the church we heard a faint sound we couldn't identify, when our pre-teen son said "My fly just pulled apart." Now what were we to do? The pastor called his tailor and we rushed over. Thankfully the tailor put in a new zipper quickly, and we just got back to the church in time to start him down the aisle.

By the time our last child's wedding was over, our son-in-law quipped, "Now that we've just gotten the hang of weddings, they are all over!"

At my husband's brother's wedding, we were all waiting at the door they were to come out. Someone handed me a pound bag of rice that I was to distribute to the others when, suddenly, here they came! No time to give any away, so I just opened the bag and tossed it all on them. Later when his brother was telling of their wedding he said, "Some idiot threw a whole bag of rice on us at once!" I confessed it was I, and explained what had happened.

EVERY DAY BRINGS SURPRISES AT THE LAKE
By Patti Bennett

My favorite lovely spot is Cedar Cove on the outskirts of Grove, Okla. Grand Lake encircles this peaceful cove on three sides. Within moments of arriving, a tranquil feeling envelops my whole being. There's something magical about the serenity and silence there. It's a time to unwind and commune with nature. Gulls, long-legged egrets, mallard and wood ducks, hummingbirds, bluebirds and woodpeckers hover around the lake. Gray squirrels gather acorns and hickory nuts while chipmunks scurry around.

Every season brings its own specialty. Autumn days are breathtaking. Everyone waits in anticipation of the arrival of the pelicans with their gigantic orange beaks to feed on the bounty of fish and chad.

Occasionally one can glimpse eagles perched on the oak and sycamore branches. Then the shimmering moon, galaxy of stars and the Milky Way can be seen for miles in the sooty, velvet sky. In the winter, the heated fish house is full of people waiting for a nibble on their lines. Other anglers line the lake in thermal-lined clothing. A catch of crappie, catfish or bass bring smiles.

In spring, pink and white dogwoods and redbuds inspire. Sounds of laughter are heard on the spring breezes. Fishermen jigging on small boats are seen on the lake. Sights and sounds are accentuated - tree frogs, owls, cicadas and boat motors. Tiny yellow and purple wildflowers enliven the scraggly grass; wild roses and foliage bloom here and there around the lake.

Summertime means a time to hike, swim, water ski, picnic or tan. The special July Fourth celebration draws everyone for barbecues, watermelon and homemade ice cream. Chats with friendly folks in the cove are fun. Gorgeous sunsets of mauve, lavender and orange awe everyone. I feel grateful to relish the moments and enjoy not doing—just being. I can hardly wait for the sunrise and the surprises a new day brings.

BATTER UP
By Gloria Williams

Oh, how I loved to play baseball. Any time we could round up enough to play, we'd have a team in a vacant lot. I had my own ball, bat, and glove. I finally gave it to our 3rd son, who worked with kids, for his team.

At church we young people liked nothing better than to play against the adults. At church camps we'd have big games. I loved batting, short stop, or first base. I was always getting sunburned, as we'd play all afternoon. I wasn't much on watching a game, as I wanted to play it. There is nothing like batting players in, catching a fly, or hitting a home run.

We had four children all playing in different towns so I had to arrange rides for them. I said kids needed three parents to take them to the games. We lived in a small town that had a women's team. I joined it at forty! We'd practice once a week and play once a week. Sometimes I had to almost crawl upstairs to bed.

Now my grandchildren are playing t-ball, or going to ball practice. They are fun to watch.

BORN AT HOME
By Donna Whittaker

I was due on Christmas and my mother planned to call me Carol. Yes, I would have been Christmas Carol. But I waited to make my arrival until a Saturday night in January. My mother planned to "stand up" at her sister Bernice's wedding in Kansas.

Instead she spent the afternoon in labor. At 6 p.m. I was delivered by our small town doctor, Dr. Starks, in a three-room Buchanan County house without electricity or running water. My grandmother and one of my Aunt Margarets boiled the water on the wood stove. When I emerged into this world, they placed a dresser drawer on a straight chair between the wood stove and the wall. Then they bundled me in soft blankets in the drawer to shield me from the winter drafts of the uninsulated house. When I was six weeks old, we moved next door to a two-story farmhouse with electricity. Indoor water didn't come into my life for another 14 years.

I was a healthy hearty baby, but my parents did not get any sleep for months. I was awake all day and cried all night. A St. Joseph pediatrician said I had too much energy and did not require much sleep. No wonder my parents had no more children and I was destined to be an only child.

Since I wasn't born on Christmas, I was not called Carol. Instead I was one of four Donnas in my class at Gower school. And, Aunt Bernice never forgot my birthday and I never forgot her wedding anniversary.

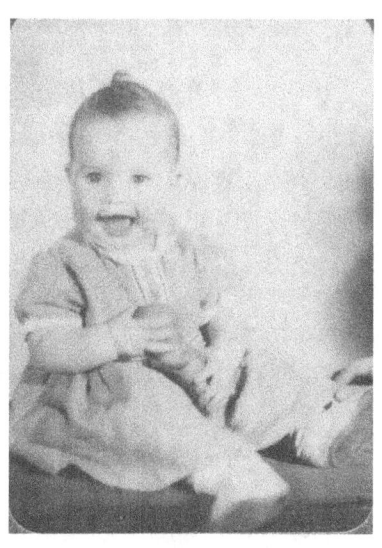

Donna Lee Reeves Whittaker

Leonard Kay Musser, Sr. and Bernice Reynolds Musser

HOPES FOR BASIC THINGS
By Patti Bennett

Being over 70 years of age, I often reflect on my hopes and dreams. I don't dream of material things. I don't hope to someday be wealthy, just to have enough money to survive. I do dream of-continued health. I love to walk and be active, and I hope to be able to stay mentally alert so I can enjoy spending time with friends and family for many more years.

I also want good eyesight, so I can read and enjoy the changing seasons, and good hearing so I'm able to listen to music and enjoy the sound of laughter. I want to be a good role model for my family and friends. I want to leave a legacy when it's my time to join my Creator, and I want the world to be a better place.

My greatest hope and dream, however, is for my son, who has lymphoma. I hope he returns to good health so he can raise his teenage son—watch him graduate, get married, have a successful career, and become a father. I want my son to enjoy the rewards of being a grandparent someday. That is what I hope—and pray—for each and every day.

MEMOIRS FROM THE DRIVE-IN MOVIES
By Jill Perkins

Growing up in the Fifties, I remember lots of visits to the drive-in movies. But I'm not going to give you the fluffy, nostalgic, candy coated version. I'm going to give it to you straight, tell you exactly how it really was. Back then, our hometown of St. Joseph, MO had three drive-ins to choose from. They were: The Belt, The Skylark, and The Cow Town. They had to be the muggiest, most mosquito infested tracks of land in the entire city.

I remember viewing these movies from the back seat of my daddy's 1951 Desoto, a very classy family car at the time. We would arrive at the Drive-In early, our goal being to get our choice of the parking spaces. Daddy would drive around and around the dusty graveled lot until we all succumbed to fits of coughing, or he found his ideal space. He always chose a space up toward the front of the lot. There were usually plenty of good ones to choose from there. Most cars would be parked in the back rows. For the life of me, I could not imagine why anyone would be so stupid as to actually choose to park in the back row.

Once The Spot was decided upon, Daddy had to situate the Desoto on the little mound that was part of each space. Since the view from the front seat and the view from the back seat were at different levels, it took some time to set the car just right for the most optimal viewing for both. Sometimes, Daddy would rock back and forth over the little mound for ten or more minutes. We'd be just about ready to "toss our cookies", before he gave up and decided that if he could see, then we could too.

Our 1951 Desoto presented yet another opposition to optimal viewing, the hood ornament. Nowadays, cars don't really have hood ornaments, and if they do, they're flat. But in the fifties, they were huge towering, artistic statues that were meant to make a statement about the individual model of car. The bigger and badder the car, the more outlandish the hood ornament would be. The Desoto had one of the largest. It was a very wide, big-headed Spanish Conquistador, decked out with a full battle helmet. There it sat, in all its frightening glory, right square in the middle of the view out the front window.

With the car finally perfectly perched on the mound, it was time to reel in the speaker. You always said a prayer that this particular speaker was working well. If it wasn't working, we'd be off driving around in the dusty lot, and starting all over again. In our family, there was quite a ritual in regards to the speaker. "I believe," my daddy told us, "it came from the Bible. 'The movie speaker must enter the vehicle through the driver side window, and can only be controlled by the male head of the household.' So it is written, so let it be." This chauvinistic attitude must have been the precursor to today's male dominance over the television remote control.

It did not matter what the movie was about. It was always parent's choice. That was okay with us. For us children, going to the Drive-In was all about the popcorn. Popcorn was Mama's domain. She made the best. She popped it up at home in an old cast iron skillet. She melted real butter all over it. It was carried to the Drive-In in a doubled brown paper grocery sack. She brought along smaller lunch sacks to serve it in. We'd wash it down with ice water from an old crockery picnic jug, served in brightly colored aluminum tumblers. It was the best. No one gave a thought back then to how badly it would clog our arteries. We just thought it was the food of the Gods, manna from heaven.

The real adventure in going to the Drive-In movies was the goings on in the back seat. Just imagine; four hyperactive, naughty children, two boys and two girls, stuffed like sardines, in the back seat of a 1951 Desoto. It was hot and sultry, and there was never enough room. The challenge literally grew with each passing year. It was a constant dog-eat-dog battle for sibling supremacy in the back seat. Sometimes it was the boys against the girls, but more often, it was every man for himself. It Was War!

The fighting was loud and violent. We fought over everything: who would get the privilege of sitting by a window and who would not? It never really mattered, there were no good spots in the back seat. If someone's bare skin touched another's, the threat of catching "cooties", was the original bacterial warfare. It did not enter our little heads, that there was absolutely no way to avoid this threat with four kids in the back seat.

There were many complaints, the most popular was, "Mama, he's looking at me. Make him stop." Poor Mama, she had to hand back four bags of popcorn at once. One at a time, and it would be demolished in mid air before it had a chance to make it to the back seat.

The four of us learned to sharpen our skills in the use of many back seat battle implements. Punching, prodding, poking, pinching, scratching, kicking, and biting were used in mass. There was a continuous air raid of round after round of projectile flying popcorn. It always took days to clear away the debris from the battlefield; I mean, the back seat of the car.

My personal favorite battle implement, and the one I was most skilled at, was my high decimal, ear piercing, sonic boom scream. This never failed to get me attention inside and out of the car. It would bring the battle to a temporary halt, allowing me precious time to rethink my strategies. But it would bring the wrath of Dad down on us for sure. I can still hear his disciplinary warning: "If I hear another blood curdling scream from the back seat, and you're not dead or dying, you will be."

During these battles, we took no prisoners, but there were casualties. There were always a number of bruised ribs, blackened eyes, and bloody noses. There would be fits of sobbing, even if the movie was not a tear jerker. The length of these wars usually lasted through the first feature, intermission, and well into the second feature. War sometimes is long and arduous.

By the end of the second feature, all sides having exhausted themselves, peace would miraculously be declared. Each sibling would fall asleep with his or her head resting on his or her sibling's back. Daddy would drive home, in peace, with a back seat full of pajama-clad little angels, covered in buttered popcorn.

Looking back, I find I'm totally perplexed. How could two apparently normal, sane, adults put themselves through this horrendous ordeal, over, and over again and all in the name of entertainment? It's beyond me. Something good did come out of those back seat wars. When I was in high school, I finally learned just what the big attraction was on the back row of the drive-in movie. I had expected free passes or maybe free candy. Boy, was that a big disappointment! I was most grateful of my expertise in battle. It was a comforting help to know I could still bloody a nose, or blacken an eye, if I had to.

SCRAPBOOKING
By Gloria Williams

I have several shelves in the basement with scrapbooks that cover 100 years. I counted the other day and there were 83. If anyone needs a name, date, picture or event, I have it!

It all began simply—nothing fancy like today's scrapbooks, just a scrapbook with pictures and memorabilia. It is a library of our lives.

First there were our baby books, school years, dating, wedding, our children's baby books (4) and grand-children's books (8). (I even did a few modern scrapbooks, but it was too expensive for me.) It began to snowball, I did one of each of our families, the places we'd lived (33), cars we'd had, and churches we'd served. Then I had scrapbooks of our vacations, our 25th, 40th and 50th anniversaries.

The grandchildren's books grew to 4 each and they loved to look at them and remember what we did and where we went and how they'd grown! When churches celebrate, they remember my scrapbooks and call me for programs or speakers they had. I have two long time pen pals (over 65 yrs). We have met a few times in NY and PA. I can write about nostalgia and have pictures to prove it I can even make a bit of cash.

I began to branch out to other types of scrapbooking like of famous people: Minnie Pearl, whom I have met, and Dr. Seuss to whom I have written. I have articles from newspapers about Roy Rogers, Red Skeleton, Shirley Temple, Helen Keller, Fibber McGee, etc. I did one of inspirational people like a woman born without arms that typed with her toes and diapered her baby with her feet. One for the boy who was born without his right hand, but became a baseball pitcher. And one for the man with fingers numb and fused together, yet he became a piano virtuoso. I made one of cute sayings and articles for speeches. Yes, there is one of my favorite recipes, and one of world events like the Oklahoma bombing, 9-11-01 and the tsunami. I can spend an interesting day leafing through our lives or being inspired by others' accomplishments. I used to think if there was a flood, or storm I would save our baby books or wedding books, but now there are too many to save! It has been a fun hobby and useful and I'll let the next generation worry about what to do with them.

LIVES WITH BELIEF OF PAYING IT FORWARD
By Patti Bennett

My way of helping others is to pay it forward! I began living with this motto two years ago, after my son died of cancer. It began when a friend asked me for a piece of his clothing, something special to me. The article of clothing came back as a memory bear, and I loved it.

I then decided to make one myself. My old Singer hadn't been used for years, but it worked to make two different bears from Kansas City Chiefs shirts, because my son loved the Chiefs.

When my friend encouraged me to sew memory bears for a local hospice, I joined a group and did just that. People provided favorite shirts, blouses, or robes of loved ones, and we cut, sewed, and stuffed them, and then returned the bears to hospice.

Most families I have never met, but just knowing I have helped others who are grieving is gratifying. Receiving the memory bear from my friend helped me, and I know the memory bears I make help others. To date, my old sewing machine has stitched more than 50 colorful bears.

William Faulkner said, "It is the writer's privilege to help mankind endure by lifting his heart." I can say the same about sewing memory bears for people who are hurting. In the case of making memory bears, there's an added bonus for me, because each time I return a finished bear to hospice, my own heart is lifted.

ON THE DAY I WAS BORN
By Jan Powell

On May 7, 1939, I came into this world. That, in itself, was not so remarkable — lots of babies were born on that day. What was remarkable was that I was one of three babies born to our mother that day, all within a thirty-minute period, and all of whom survived. And we were not in a hospital, but at home.

First came my brother, weighing six pounds, with red hair and green eyes. Boy, was my father proud and happy that the trauma was almost over. They named their son James Eddy after both grandfathers.

Just when the two doctors, Dad, and Mom were congratulating each other, I came along. Not to be outdone by my brother's dramatic entrance, I weighed in at six pounds as well, and had brown hair and brown eyes. They called me Janice.

The doctors yelled at my father to get out of the way, as they needed more room, and he immediately fainted dead away and crashed to the floor. Both doctors ignored him. My mom was told to relax and wait for the afterbirth to arrive shortly, but she was not having any of that nonsense.

Instead, she told the doctor that she felt another baby coming and, of course, she was right. Out came another beautiful baby girl, weighing in at five and a half pounds, and having blond hair and blue eyes. From that day on, Joyce, as they named her, was the Prima donna of all.

Three babies born in thirty minutes; not a bad day's work at home for my mother. My father was not thrilled at having three additions to the family to provide for, and joked that they belonged to the milkman, the mailman, and the iceman because of our different hair and eye colors. My older brother, who was two at the time, was not thrilled either; he had been willing to give up his crib for one baby, but not for three.

Jan Powell (far right) with her mother and siblings, 1939

MEMORIES OF World War II
By Gloria Williams

I was about twelve when the troop trains would go through Enid, Okla. Huge, long trains filled with guys. The churches would meet the trains with free sandwiches, cupcakes and punch. The station was crammed. Now there are no passenger trains through Enid, nor even a station.

My uncle was in the Air Force. He was the shortest one and they had him trying to light the cigarette of the tallest guy there. In fact he took some stretching exercises to even get in. He also drank lots of water and ate as many bananas as he could so he would weigh enough.

It always troubled me that the world allowed the Germans to kill so many Jews. The adults said they didn't know about it until later. News was not worldwide then and they saw it only at the movies. But my heart ached for the Jews, how badly they were treated, with entire families wiped out. How did they stand their losses, the cold, sickness, hunger, and bugs?

The world still isn't kind to many. We are still hurting one another and killing each other. It must break God's heart. It does mine.

ACTIVITY THE BEST WAY TO REMAIN YOUNG
By Patti Bennett

Exercise is the best medicine. For more than 30 years, walking has been my chosen activity. At age 70, I can see the benefits. For one thing, it keeps the arthritis at bay.

I have to push myself out the door most days, because a lot of things I really enjoy doing are sedentary activities, such as reading, writing and sewing. I live near a walking trail, so I don't have an excuse not to exercise.

When the temperatures are frigid, I go to the senior center with friends and use the treadmill, elliptical walker, and Nautilus equipment. It's a fun place to socialize.

I keep my mind active by playing dominoes, and board games such as *Rummikub*. I like *Sudoku*, crossword puzzles, and creative writing, and every week I take organ lessons. Learning the computer also challenges the mind.

It's fun to be able to do all of these things. I have found the best prescription for aging well is staying active and staying connected to people. It's a lifelong habit that enriches everyone's lives.

MY GRANDMOTHER ETHEL
By Gloria Williams

I am going to describe my grandmother on my mother's side, Ethel. I lived with her sometimes. She was only five feet tall and she hated being short, as she could never reach the top shelves and always had to climb on something.

She was a good cook. I have her recipes but they never turn out as good as hers. On Easter we had "Golden Rod Toast" with boiled sliced eggs in white sauce over toast with sieved eggs yolks on top. At Christmas we had a big sweetened popcorn cake with one candle on it for Christ's birthday. In summer we had delicious strawberry short cake.

Ethel was terribly frightened of mice. One day she called us to come quickly. When we got there she was walking on chairs (seven of them) to get to the phone! She loved to crochet and made gorgeous things. She wanted to teach me, but at ten I'd rather climb trees. At 18 when I was ready to learn, she was too old to teach me.

Her house was our home and many of us had lived there at sometime. It was an old house of two stories with closets that wound around upstairs. It was a great place to play and store "stuff". One day I planned to buy it, but it never happened. I'd go to visit her in the summer time and I always got homesick at sundown. She would try to cheer me up by making funny faces and making me laugh. She finally got Alzheimer's disease. She would shake her finger at the T.V. and tell them not to smoke in her house.

She kept a spotless house. She washed on Monday, ironed on Tuesday, etc. She even ironed the underwear! But as she grew worse she would fight us when it was her bath time.

We always went to Ethel's house for the holidays, relatives and friends. We also had company for Sunday dinners. We never missed church. But she loved "*Stella Dallas*" and when it was on, she would watch it and then be late for the women's meeting.

She loved her fluffy white, little spitz dog. Ethel was fun loving and hard working. She gave my life security.

DAUGHTER LOVED FIRST DRESS
By Patti Bennett

When I was a 20-something homemaker, my husband bought me a brand new portable Singer sewing machine. My friend and I browsed fabric shops for material to sew dresses for our preschool daughters.

Though I had not sewn since high school, I chose yellow cotton material and white daisy eyelet for a dress for my daughter. After I finished it, a neighbor knocked, collecting for a charity. My young daughter ran to the closet and excitedly said, "See what my mother made for me!"

Kelley's blue eyes sparkled as she showed off her new dress, my first homemade for her. Her delight was my reward.

In junior high, Kelley learned to sew and surprised me with an apron she had made in sewing class. She became quite the seamstress in high school and even made her prom dress. Later, after she married, I made her a quilt out of her material scraps. I appliquéd colorful butterflies on white blocks. Of course, the backing and the strips binding the blocks were canary yellow, the same color as her first homemade dress.

HAIR DO'S AND DON'TS
By Gloria Williams

Oh thank goodness for newer and better methods to curl hair than those "TORTURE" rollers hooked up to electricity, that burned your scalp. They would blow on your head and fan you, but it didn't help much. Why is that those who had curly hair, wanted straight, and vice-a-versa?

Until I was nine, my mom kept my hair curly, but when she died, I became known as that stringy haired kid. Remember when they used to think it was bad to wash your hair more than once a week? My hair got oily and awful. Hooray, now I can wash it every day, if I like.

I remember two times when I had beautiful hair. In Brazil, my neighbor liked to do my hair into a beehive. I wanted to go see Carnival—Mardi Gras. But it wasn't proper for Christians to attend. I asked the church leaders if I could go to experience their culture. They replied that I could see the parade, but it would be better not to the parties, for they danced all night, got drunk, and sometimes were almost naked.

I took a Brazilian girlfriend, so she could explain it to me. It was beautiful. I have never, seen anything like it: the costumes, the music, the steel drums, and parade. I hadn't realized they threw confetti. We were covered with it. It settled into our beehive coiffures. No way we could get it out by the next morning in time for church.

So we were like a billboard—everyone could SEE where we'd been.

The second time I had pretty hair was when the local hairdresser offered to do my hair free. (I was the pastor's wife). But I didn't go at first, for I was afraid I hadn't heard her correctly and I had no money to pay. But I finally went at her begging. I loved being spoiled; it was terrific. I hated moving away from there.

I also loved to swim, but what do you do with your hair? I perspired so in summer, especially so on my head. I never could wear a hat either, for soon I would be dripping.

I tried wigs when I had cancer, but it felt like a hat. One Sunday all went well until I got into the car and plopped down. My wig flew off my head, to the floor. I ducked down in the seat until we took off. Wigs were not for me—if I could not fix my own, I surely could not comb a wig either.

KINDNESS OUT OF ASHES
By Susan Walter

As I sipped a cup of coffee one morning, my thoughts wandered back to the time when we had no cups, no coffee, or a chair to sit on. In four hours, we were left with nothing but a car and the clothing we were wearing.

The tragedy happened on a cold, clear night in January 1969. We were enjoying a Christian choir at St. Paul Lutheran Church, when a neighborhood friend called the church. We heard the frightening words, "Your home is on fire!"

The drive home was in silence. There was comfort in the words from Matthew 28:20, "Lo, I am with you always, even unto the ends of the world."

When we arrived home, we could do nothing but watch the dense smoke spiral from the windows like great tidal waves, as the flames destroyed our home. The gushing water and the crackling of ice broke the night's silence.

We stayed with friends until we found a house to rent. Sleep was difficult that night, but we were thankful all of us were safe.

Like a learning child, we had to take a step at a time. The insurance adjuster requested an itemized list of the contents of each room. I entered the desolate structure with a pen, pad, and flashlight (the windows were already boarded up). The first thing I saw as I entered the kitchen, was the huge, blackened wall clock my husband, Norm, had designed for me. The kitchen was easy to itemize. I was familiar with everything in every drawer. After all, where else had I spent so much time cooking for the family of eight?

It was necessary to step carefully on the ice-covered floors as I shuffled from room to room. When I glanced around rooms, my vision was blurred with tears. The much-used blond sewing machine had changed to a charred grey. Our children's fingers would no longer play the big, old player piano I had nicknamed "the monster." As I touched the girls' clothing, they fell to the floor in charred heaps. The boys' mattresses soaked up the water like huge sponges. The "designed by dad" bedrooms were a big, sad mess. A memory notebook of the children's antics over the years was lost forever. It would be impossible to retain all the information in my "memory department."

As each day passed, the sunshine of love had broken through to warm our hearts. The generosity of friends unfolded unbelievably. There were dinner invitations, gas fill-ups, household items, clothing, beauty shop appointments, sewing essentials, shopping sprees, funds from the PTA that had been collected for the school library, one Sunday's church offering, and the volunteering of employees' of a roofing company to roof our new home. How blessed we were!

Out of all the kindnesses bestowed upon us, one special kindness stands out in my mind: a sweet, elderly, frail friend from our church presented us with a used coffee pot with two dollar bills tucked inside.

"This is all I have to give you," she said sadly. But to us, it was a wonderful donation. It reminded me of a passage in Mark 12:24: "A poor widow came and put two small copper coins, worth only a fraction of a cent,"

Jesus said. "The poor widow has put more into the treasury than all the others."

We moved into our new home on our twenty-fifth wedding anniversary. What a wonderful gift! A few months later, two sons were discharged from military service. Thankfulness was rooted deep in our hearts.

Out of ashes came kindnesses, and the love of our heavenly Father through the generosity of and concern of His people. We remain thankful today — for all our blessings.

Susan Walter with two of her books.

SHARED FAMILY LEGACY THROUGH QUILTS
By Patti Bennett

One of my favorite pastimes is embroidering blocks for baby quilts. I began shortly after my mother passed away. In her closet hung several colorful dresses that she enjoyed wearing around the house. She called them shifts, and they were made of straight pieces of material. Memories of my mother bustling around in them made them precious to me and I kept them.

After her granddaughter was born, I decided to make a keepsake quilt. I began embroidering pink cats on white material. Then I chose a pink plaid shift to bind the blocks together. At first, it was difficult to cut Mom's dresses into strips, but I managed to complete the task.

When her grandson was born, I cut a tan shift into strips for a train quilt. Five more grandchildren and several great-grandchildren received multicolored keepsake quilts featuring lions, seahorses, alligators, angels and zoo and farm animals.

I'm glad I found my mother's neatly pressed dresses in her closet. It's been a pleasurable pastime to create these heritage quilts. They are a legacy I can share.

DISASTER
By Gloria Williams

Around 1958, a friend in Brazil had given us a kitten. We soon discovered he had a very obnoxious disposition. He was not friendly and hissed at us a lot. We never got him toilet trained and we tried to keep him outside as much as we could.

One day, I had gone to a church meeting, taking our three-year-old son with me, and leaving the baby with my husband. After I left, he received a phone call that the director of women's work had arrived at the bus station and could he pick her up? He called me to go by and get her. Then he knew he had to get the cat out of the house quickly, but the cat had other ideas!

The cat was in the front room and he had to slide the sofa and then the chair to reach him, but the cat dashed into the bedroom where he promptly messed under the bed! My husband stopped to clean that up. Meanwhile the cat had disappeared into the kitchen behind the refrigerator. While he was trying to reach the cat, it hid under the stove. While he tried to catch the cat there, it raced to the back porch under the washer.

By now my husband was not in a good mood, nor was the cat. My husband propped up the washer to reach the cat. When the German police dog outside heard the commotion it lunged against the door, barking and bounding after the cat. The washer fell over, with water spurting everywhere. He covered it with his hand trying to think what to do next. He needed to get a ladder from the garage to get to the attic to turn off the water, but the key to the garage was in the bedroom. By the time he raced back to the porch, water was knee deep. He finally got the water off and went to check on the cat.

The dog had corralled the cat outside and they were in a big fight. The dog injured the cat so badly, my husband had to kill the cat.

About this time I arrived home with the guest. With the house a wreck, I exclaimed, "What on earth happened?" My husband simply replied," I killed the cat!"

"PLAYFUL KITTEN" Pencil drawing by Julie L. Casey

HOLIDAYS SPENT WITH STRANGERS WHO BECAME FAMILY
By Patti Bennett

There is a marvelous place in Kansas City, Missouri, called Hope Lodge, where my son, Steve, and I spent four consecutive holidays - Christmas, New Year's, Valentine's Day, and St. Patrick's Day.

Hope Lodge is located in the historic Quality Hill district and is a haven for cancer patients and their families. Lodging is free, as it is funded through donations to the American Cancer Society. Strangers with similar health problems soon become friends and even family. Hope Lodge is a home away from home, with access to kitchens, laundry rooms, computers, game rooms, a fitness room, and a large movie room complete with a selection of videos.

Each holiday Steve and I spent at Hope Lodge was special. The staff, as well as volunteers and civic groups, brought in a delicious smorgasbord of meals and desserts. In addition, they made the holidays as fun and festive as possible for those of us who were unable to be home for the holidays. What a boon it was for those undergoing chemotherapy and other treatments, as well as for their families, myself included.

As the Christmas holiday neared, the staff at Hope Lodge decorated trees, brought in cookies and punch, and entertained us with parties, games and music—all in an effort to make our stay as "normal" and memorable as possible. What a caring staff.

In April - the day before Easter—Steve lost his 17-month battle to lymphoma. Our new friends, with whom we had shared recent holidays, supported our family with hugs, compassion, warm sentiments, and encouragement for our son's own Resurrection Day.

Those so-called strangers from Hope Lodge became part of our family during the holidays - and one of the toughest times of our lives.

MERRY CHRISTMAS, DARLING
By Jill Perkins

It was Christmastime, 1969. I had graduated from high school the previous spring and was working part-time to pay my tuition into nursing school. It would be starting in the spring. My high school sweetheart, Ronnie, and I had talked about the possibility of a wedding down the line. It would have been a perfect holiday season except for one thing. The United States of America was engaged in a bloody war in South Vietnam. And for the last six months, so was my fiancé, Ronnie.

The war had been going on for some time. Though I was aware of the war, it had not touched me here in the comfort and safety of my mid-American home. That is, not until that year. Having a loved one off in the midst of the war had a frightening way of bringing the fighting to your own front door.

Ronnie's mom had promised him a box of homemade cookies every week that he was away. She enlisted me into the "Cookie Baking Corps." Most Saturdays I'd rise early and walk the two blocks up the street to Ronnie's house. His mom and I would bake enough cookies to fill a huge box. Mom and I were fast becoming great friends. She made just baking cookies so much fun. We'd share the work, some girl talk, and laughter. Lots and lots of laughter. Ronnie wrote home that he shared cookies with the other GIs in his platoon. It seemed homemade cookies were in big demand in South Vietnam.

That year, our holidays were not going very well. The first week in November, we received word that Ronnie's platoon had gone on a mission into Cambodia. They had found several men from the platoon dead, but the rest of the platoon was listed as MIA, missing in action. Naturally, we were frightened. We clung to each other and we clung to hope. Hope that Ronnie and his platoon would be found soon and found alive. But with each passing week, fear grew and hope dwindled.

Mom and I continued to bake and mail cookies every week. It was an unspoken message between us: to stop would be to admit that Ronnie was not coming back home.

That year, Karen Carpenter of the Carpenters recorded "Merry Christmas, Darling." Its lyrics were about a couple separated and missing each other at Christmas. I had a copy of the 45-rpm record. I'd play it over and over until it was worn thin. Each time I played it, I'd sob with sickening grief. I didn't know for sure why I kept doing it; I just felt compelled to. Maybe I thought if I punished myself with the song enough, God would somehow look down on Ronnie, wherever he was, and save him. People do strange, unrealistic things when in the throngs of fear and grief.

Christmas Eve was on Saturday. I dutifully trudged up the hill to bake cookies. Mom and I tried our best to share the Christmas spirit. She was being joyful for my sake, and I was being cheerful for hers. We did the best we could. After all, we knew we were just one family among many Americans with loved ones away fighting in the war that year.

When the last batch of cookies went into the oven, Mom said, "Let's take a break." She poured us a cup of coffee and we sat down at the kitchen table. Suddenly, Mom's eyes were misty and she'd gotten all emotional.

For a brief second, fear's cold fingers gripped my heart. Mom reached into her apron pocket and pulled out a small box. It was wrapped in bright Christmas paper and tied with a red bow. I breathed a sigh of relief as she handed it to me. She then revealed that, months ago, Ronnie had sent her money to buy me a Christmas present. He'd told her the exact item and the only store to get it at.

I started to tremble and cry as I opened up Ronnie's long-distance Christmas present. It was exquisite. It was a silver medallion watch on a long neck chain. Watches like that were one of the most popular gifts that Christmas of '69, though how Ronnie knew that all the way from South Vietnam was a mystery. But on the other hand, it was so like him. As I stared in awestruck wonder at my gift, Mom told me to turn it over. Ronnie had told her to have it engraved. Turning it over, I read, "Yours For All Time." Then my tears really started to flood my face.

As Mom and I sat there at the table, admiring Ronnie's good taste in jewelry, we were aware of heavy-booted footsteps on the front porch. It was about time the for postman to get there. Mom and I were discussing whether I should put on my new watch now or wait until I had cleaned all the cookie makings I had smeared down the front of me. We had laughed all morning at each other because of all the cookies that had ended up all over us, instead of in the box destined for our boys in Vietnam.

Suddenly, we heard a deep voice behind us. "Put it on now. I can't wait to see how you look with it on."

We would have known that voice anywhere. Two very happy women, screaming and crying with joy, jumped up and ran to embrace their soldier, nearly knocking each other over.

Ronnie dropped his duffle bag to the floor, spread out his arms and pulled us both into his chest. Time stood still as the three of us laid kisses all over each other's faces. Tears running down from three pairs of eyes, mingled together.

He looked a bit pale and thinner in his dress uniform, but to me, he'd never looked so wonderful and handsome. He wasn't dead in Cambodia. He wasn't missing in action. He was very much alive and right here now, dripping melted snow from his boots onto Mom's kitchen floor.

Finally Ronnie pleaded, "Say girls, do you think you could stop the mushy stuff and get that sheet of cookies out of the oven before they burn up? What's a soldier got to do to get some milk and cookies around here?"

We got Ronnie sitting comfortably in his dad's recliner, the best chair in the house by far. He was provided with a plate of warm cookies and a big glass of cold milk. Mom and I went back to the kitchen to clean up our mess.

About this time, Nina, Ronnie's eight-year-old sister, came home from skating at the roller rink. She casually said "hi" to Ronnie. Dropping her skates on the living room rug, she headed straight to the kitchen, guided by the smell of fresh-baked cookies. She slipped across the floor and slid into a kitchen chair, grabbing cookies as she did so.

"Mom," she calmly said around the cookie in her mouth, "Ronnie's not in 'Bodia like you said. He's in there, sitting in Daddy's chair. And if he spills something on it, or he don't get out of it before Daddy gets home, won't there be hell to pay? That's what you always tell me!"

In spite of Nina's cussing, Mom and I rocked the kitchen walls with our laughter. We laughed until we could hardly breathe, and our sides threatened to split. Nina's childlike mind had not registered the shock of seeing her big brother in the living room, eating cookies. But in all fairness, we had shielded the child from the dangerous situation Ronnie's platoon had been in. We both knew for a fact that Dad would be thrilled beyond words to come home and find his "missing in action" son sitting in his chair, even if Ronnie spilled milk all over it. We couldn't wait to see the look on Dad's face when he got home from work.

This was going to be a perfect Christmas after all. No present that Santa could ever put under the tree could be better or more loved than having Ronnie home for Christmas, safe and sound. It would be a Christmas none of us would ever forget.

Later, when Ronnie and I could steal a few moments alone, he told me a little about Cambodia. It was very difficult for him. He revealed that the platoon had been dug-in and penned down by enemy fire for weeks. They lost track of time. Many GIs had been killed and even more were left with disabling injuries. Ronnie had been one of the few "lucky ones." He told me he felt very guilty. He could not understand why so many good men were dead, and he wasn't. I didn't like hearing him talk like this, but I knew he needed to get it off his chest. I just held him tight and let him talk.

Ronnie told how they were able to get Christmas music broadcast over a small radio one of the GIs had. They would all draw close together around the tiny radio. The volume had to be low, but that little radio was like a lifeline to the rest of the world. There must have been a base somewhere nearby playing Christmas music from the US.

Ronnie told me he kept hearing a new Christmas song from the Carpenters. Did I remember the Carpenters? Of course I did! Ronnie had taken me to Kansas City to see them in concert. Ronnie said the song made him think about me. It had kept him hanging in there, determined to somehow make it home again.

"You don't have to tell me about that song," I said. "I played it over and over. It got me through this time also."

Ronnie could only look at me with his mouth agape; he was so amazed. "Just imagine," he finally declared. "A song over the radio kept two people in love, united in spirit and bonded together, even though they were separated by half a world and a bloody war! It was, without a doubt, a real Christmas miracle."

He pulled me into his arms and held me like he'd never let me go. Looking up into his eyes, I had just one thing to say:

"Merry Christmas, Darling."

IN THE SHADOWS OF GREATNESS
By Marianne Brachman

As I was growing up in Waukegan, Illinois, the ravines were well known for their lushness and meandering paths along much of the city on Lake Michigan. These ravines were our playgrounds, hiding places, and gave us an early education about nature, geography, and poverty. A particular ravine was featured prominently in native son, Ray Bradbury's, fiction stories of *Green Town* and his name was often mentioned as if he were a family member. The discussion might go, "Oh, Ray Bradbury... this and that!".

As a child, we lived across the red-bricked street from the former Bradbury family home along St. James, Washington, and Glen Rock streets. He was considered an old neighbor that had moved on years ago, but brought pride to our town, unlike a serial killer who had gripped the city in fear years ago. Bradbury's literary shadow was as large as that of another native son, Jack Benny.

While the public library grabbed hold of Bradbury's fame for various book-related festivals, the entertainment and academic worlds claimed Mr. Benny as their Waukegan "patron and namesake." A large statue of Jack Benny was erected in our downtown and it was a rite of passage to have your photo taken next to him. The school, arts center, and festivals keep his legacy, humor, and humbleness alive. His family home has long been demolished and yet his influence on arts and the fabric of this city is still amazingly strong.

As if two local talents were not enough, Vincent Price, an accomplished actor, had been reported to have lived in Waukegan on Grand Avenue in a Victorian mansion many years before and the folklore was that the house was haunted and was avoided at Halloween, especially.

Football was not to be left behind and Waukegan produced at least two well-known players, Otto Graham and Paul Adams. Baseball had a few guys, but football was what Waukegan East Campus High School was proud of and known for.

One weekend, the local newspaper highlighted the Nugent family in Waukegan, whose son, a U.S. Marine, had made an exceptionally good marriage proposal, because the prospective bride's parents were coming to meet the family. Luci Baines Johnson was photographed as radiant as was Lady Bird Johnson and LBJ, along with their carloads of Secret Service agents in Waukegan for an engagement lunch like no other. This presidential visit was the talk of the town for the next decade.

Neither of my parents was born in Waukegan, but my younger sister, Arlene Francis, and I were, and we were considered "locals" which gave me a sense of pride I retain strongly today. I moved away from Waukegan, Illinois for college and marriage and, yet, I think back upon so many aspects of my life there, living in the shadows of ravines, authors, ball players, politicians, and regular folk. I go back every year to the cemetery, park, and downtown. It is too painful to go back to the family home, or red-bricked street at St. James and Glen Rock, but in my dreams I am sitting on the cement steps and life is good in Waukegan.

OUR BARN
By Gloria Williams

Our barn was the largest building on the farm. It was unpainted. It was where we put the twin calves, which were born outside in the winter and had gotten the tips of their ears frozen, where we pitched the hay in the loft, and where we milked our three cows.

We kids used to play in the hay mound and so did the kittens. We rigged up a rope whereby we could swing off and land in the hay. One day the hay was a bit sparse and I jumped and landed on a nail in a board. Out came mom to get it off my bare foot and apply kerosene. It healed fine.

The barn had a sloped roof of tin on a shed, and I have no idea why, but my brother and I decided to ride the scooter there. It had a barn door cut in half. The bottom was shut, but the top was blowing and banging in the wind. My brother fell off, and I ran to get mom. His leg had been broken. We were in big trouble! It seemed ages that he had to walk on crutches.

Dad kept a barrel of old molasses to put over the cows oats while we milked them. We found out it tasted pretty good. I wonder how clean it was now.

One time I was milking on a one-legged stool. The flies were bad and the cow stomped her foot and somehow put her foot in my coverall pocket, which spilled the milk and me.

One Sunday evening we had company, and four of us kids decided to see who could catch the most flies in our milk bucket. I won, but not with mom, and the milk had to be given to the pigs. We also fed the cats by squirting milk in their mouths as they stood on their hind legs begging.

The windmill was next to the barn with a big tank of water. It was refreshing to take a dip in it on a hot day. Once a hailstorm hit just as we were going to the house from milking. We grabbed a couple of buckets to put over our heads. Wow, what a noise the hail made hitting the buckets!

Today the barn is gone and the ground all plowed. I can barely tell where it has been.

"BARN" Photo by James Fly

SPRING IS A TIME FOR ALL TO ENJOY
By Patti Bennett

More than any other season, spring enlivens me as Mother Nature stirs from winter's slumber. To defy snowflakes, dull brown bulbs planted in autumn emerge as gold or lavender crocus, scarlet tulips, and yellow daffodils. Soon forsythia, lilacs, dogwoods, and redbuds bloom in all their glory. Gentle rains bring blossoms and buds, promising flowers and fruit to come. Lettuce, radishes, and sugar-snap peas are a prelude to tasty summertime vegetables. Red-breasted robins pull earthworms from patches of emerald grass and herald wrens and orioles busily building nests. Even animals give new life with the arrival of lambs, calves, chicks, and foals.

People smile as they shed winter coats and don light jackets to spade gardens, wash windows, hunt morel mushroom delicacies, or grab fishing poles or walking shoes. Energetic children, welcoming the balmy breezes, jump on skateboards or bikes, and laughter fills the air.

Spring also ushers in favorite holidays—Easter, Mother's Day, Memorial Day, and Father's Day. Spring spells newness, growth, and transformation. Peoples' spirits soar like kites, fluttering in the bright blue skies amid the white fluffy clouds. Yes, the aliveness and freshness of spring saunters in for all to enjoy.

SUMMERTIME HAS SEVERAL REWARDS
By Patti Bennett

I love summertime, except for the humidity, which is a part of the season. I cope by getting up earlier to garden, mow, walk, or bake. I use the slow cooker and microwave to make meals. Eating out at restaurants, grilling, picnics in the park, and homemade ice cream make the summer more tolerable.

Summer spells outdoor fun, such as ballgames, horseshoes, and family reunions. I also enjoy the gentle breeze under the shade trees or visiting with friends and neighbors on the front porch or patio.

I enjoy the delectable pleasure that only early morning brings. In the afternoon, I enjoy resting in the air conditioning. I read, sew, or watch television.

I relish the longer days of summer, though often they are sticky or sweltering. Summer has its rewards, which help me bear Missouri.

EXCITEMENT OF AUTUMN ENLIVENS ALL
By Patti Bennett

To me, autumn is an awesome season. It means glorious trees aflame, chrysanthemums bursting with vibrancy and honking geese flying south in V-formation. I enjoy going to football games, going on hayrides and brisk walks.

I love the harvest-time bounty, with apple picking, pumpkin carving, and walnut hulling. I have renewed energy with the change of pace, and I return to doing extra things, such as washing windows and winterizing.

Autumn means back to school for children and adults. Since I live in a college town, I take advantage of continuing education classes. In previous falls, I enjoyed photography and adult fitness classes.

I like the longer evenings, with more time indoors to read and sew, with the fireplace aglow on chilly nights. I relish oven-baked meals, hot chocolate, popcorn balls, and apple dumplings.

Excitement builds as I look forward to costumed goblins on Halloween and decorating for the upcoming winter holidays. Autumn enlivens all of Missouri.

WINTER'S JOYS INCLUDE RELAXING BY FIRE
By Patti Bennett

Winter has become one of my closest friends. During this chilly season, I appreciate being cozy inside with extra time to read, write, sew, play music, and just putter around the house. Even cleaning a closet or drawer sounds like fun.

For a short season, gardening, mowing, raking, and yard work cease. Nature needs a rest and so do I. Sparkling snowflakes falling on the spaded garden spot and ice glistening on tree branches are gratifying. Still, I don't relish driving on icy streets.

In winter, there's time to cook new casseroles or soups with okra and tomatoes I have in the freezer from my summer garden. It's time to enjoy family during the holidays, and New Year's Day is a time to reflect on new beginnings and resolutions.

Longer evenings are a time for relaxing. For me, pleasant evenings involve watching a glowing fireplace and sipping hot tea or cocoa while embroidering a quilt block or perusing a seed catalog as thoughts turn toward spring. However, spring can wait. I would like to see those frigid days linger a while longer.

ON THE DAY I WAS BORN
By Jill Perkins

On the Day I was born, April 9th, 1951, my brother was born right behind me with great unexpectation. Not expecting twins, the subject of names became a huge quandary, except for my grandma. Months before, she had predicted twins, a boy and a girl that she called Jack and Jill. No one had paid her any attention; after all, she was very old and quite lost in dementia. But that was who we became: Jack and Jill.

From our birth on, someone was always reading to us from *The Big Book of Mother Goose Rhymes*. Long before I could speak, I knew, my conscious thoughts spilled out of my mind in the form of rhythm and rhyme. At school when I became capable of writing words that were legible, my future was never a mystery to me: I was born to write poetry!

MY AUNT HELEN
By Mary Jane Fields

Every family, honest enough to admit it has an Aunt Helen, or maybe it's an Uncle Joe. My Aunt Helen is one of my mother's younger sisters. My grandmother had ten children: five boys and five girls. The oldest and youngest boys died as very young children, but grandma raised a couple of 'strays' so it was a very full house.

I never called my aunts and uncles, 'Aunt or 'Uncle', only by their first names or nicknames. I meant no disrespect, that's just the way it was. Aunt Becky and Aunt Minnie were my great aunts, and they had earned their titles somehow, unbeknownst to me. That's just the way it was.

Sometimes Helen's brothers and sisters called her "Hellie", a name well deserved. All her siblings had nicknames: Mary Naomi, my mother, was "Sister"; Winifred Clarissa, "Joan" (she picked that); William Jackson, "Bill"; Beulah Carma, "Beulie"; Emery Leland, "Jim"; Faith Jane, "Toots"; Edward Rushworth, "Bud".

Helen was the fun character of the family, ready and willing for anything mischievous. She was very limber and could do all sorts of what was called acrobatics. She also might be heard calling down from the roof, the top of the windmill, or a limb of a tree. She was generous, almost to a fault. She never had much in earthly goods but she would gladly share it all with anyone. She was a hard worker, willing to undertake anything that didn't eat her first, with no thought of the consequence.

Helen had a great sense of humor and was my

favorite fun aunt. I loved her and I felt that she loved me. She did have one weakness, which became one big fault: booze. Next to booze, came cigarettes. This started with grape leaves behind the barn and escalated from there. When she drank, she no longer was my favorite fun aunt. You were never quite sure who she might be, as different quantities, qualities, or wind directions might determine what attitude she developed. I knew one thing, for sure: none were ones I wanted to be around.

On one occasion during a Saturday night party at Grandma's (Grandma didn't drink but she was outnumbered by offspring that did), Helen got on a mad drunk, focusing on her husband, Barney. Demonstrating great wisdom, she went across the road and threw her wedding ring into the raspberry patch. This made for an interesting Sunday morning group activity. The ring was found!

She was not blessed with children but married Barney who had a 4-year-old daughter, Audrey. Helen never called her "my daughter", ever! She was referred to as "Barney's girl" or "the girl I raised", which was a poor choice of words because Audrey pretty much raised herself while doing all the work and babysitting Helen.

In the early 1940s, during World War II, there were few male members of the family around to manage and work on Grandma's truck farm or to sell cars on my Uncle Bud's used car lot. Helen helped with both. She was an excellent driver and went along with the men hired by Bud to drive used cars back from Chicago. I suspect they were black-marketed, as cars were not being manufactured and used ones were at a premium. I do know that sometimes they smuggled black market sugar back in those cars, much as hard drugs are being smuggled today, and we welcomed the sugar, just as the drugs are welcomed today.

Once, after they stopped at the edge of Chicago for supper before starting the long non-stop trip back to St. Joseph, about 50 miles out along the dark highway, Helen heard something in the back seat. Startled, she screamed as she was driving solo, of course, and the something sat up. You didn't lock cars in those days. A drunk had crawled into the back seat to sleep it off in comfort while they were eating. She stopped the car and set him out along the highway to hitch his own way back to Chicago.

I spent my summers working out in the fields at ten cents an hour. My least favorite task was liming cucumbers. To do this, you have a gunny sack, and put as much lime as you can handle in it, because you don't want to walk back to the shed for refills. It's hot. Carry the lime-filled sack down to the cucumber patch and shake this lime onto the plants. I repeat, it's hot—not perspiration hot, sweaty hot. There's no shade. You're in the middle of a 35-acre field of various vegetables, and it's hot. You cannot stop breathing, so you breathe in lime dust. That is not a pleasant experience. Then your sweat runs. If you reach up to divert it, presto: more lime dust. As I said, it was my least favorite job.

A cooler, and perhaps more interesting summer job, took place at night. The field hands would prepare the rusting pickup for market. The various produce would be put in bushel baskets, half-bushel baskets, or pecks as needed. About 10 o'clock at night, it was time for the trip to the Kansas City Market. Remember, there was a shortage of men and they couldn't work all day and go to market at night. Helen was a good driver and at 14, I was allowed, or drafted, to help her.

All set, our trip's first stop was always at the south end of the Belt Highway, which in those days was way out of town. There she'd have a beer or two and I'd have a Coke and be given some nickels for the Juke Box. There was no Interstate 29, as Eisenhower [who developed the interstate system] hadn't been elected yet. If we went down highway 169, the next stop was Gower's bar. Here she had more beer and I might have had an ice cream cone. Next stop, Grayson, then Smithville. By this time, I could not possibly think of another Coke, but to her, the beer was only getting better. It was a pretty straight non-stop trip to the market and by this time we needed to hurry, as the market opened at 2:00 a.m. There was the immediate need for a potty stop, which had to be made behind a dark roadside bush or tree. If it truly was an emergency, bush, tree, and dark suddenly become non-essentials.

At the market, we would find a stall, probably not a good one, as we would be late and the good ones would be taken. If she was able, she would back the truck into a stall, lie down across the seat of the pickup, and go to sleep. If backing was a skill she had temporarily lost, usually some other trucker would handle it. I was only 14, too young to drive. Aunt Helen would sleep until morning. I would sell off the load, hire the shaggers to deliver what is not taken cash and carry, and repack what had not sold, in preparation for a much quicker trip back to St. Joseph.

When our tomatoes ripened, everyone's tomatoes ripened. As a result of this, we often hauled unsold tomatoes back home. A couple of trips and they were ready to be sold, with tomato juice dripping through the now-stained basket and, in some cases, a bit of mold peeking out. These went to Otoe Canning Company in Nebraska City. I never bought any Otoe brand, ever.

To her dying day, Aunt Helen believed that jackalopes existed and that she had seen a pig climb a tree in Arkansas. Even with all her smokin' and drinkin' and cussin' (she could do that too), she outlived all her nine brothers and sisters. At her funeral, during our last look at an aunt we dearly loved, my daughter and I slipped a cigarette in her casket. We weren't sure she'd need matches so we didn't include those.

THE DIVINE BEAUTY OF WINTER
By Susan Walter

"God saw what He had made, and, behold, IT WAS VERY GOOD." Genesis 1:13.

Jack Frost has finished his lacy designs on windows, the pumpkins are tired of their broad smiles and autumn has crept to the doorway of winter — the season of crisp splendor. Winter is the season when the earth is sometimes cloaked with ensembles of white. God's handiwork is displayed everywhere. The snow-dipped evergreens are swaying in the slight breeze while the snow-clad housetops glisten like the nighttime stars. The shade of the country church casts shadows on the bed of white, as the snowdrifts continue to pile high against God's house of worship. The snowflakes twirl as softly as baby's lullaby.

The crimson sun peeks through the white and grey floating clouds against a delicate blue backdrop, making sparkling diamonds on the blankets of cotton-like snow.

Needles from the aged pine trees prick through the snow-covered limbs to form little white porcupines sleeping on the branches. The delicate lacy snowflakes, pushed by a whisper of a breeze, keep parachuting hither and yon. God's winter show is closing for the day. Dusk, the dim part of twilight, comes all too quickly. How blessed we are to have the warmth of our homes. The smoke from the chimneys begins tying grey ribbons in the sky. Winter has gone to sleep.

"God saw what He had made, and, behold IT WAS VERY GOOD." Genesis 1:13.

"COUNTRY CHURCH" Painting by Susan Walter

MOM WAS A BASEBALL LEGEND
By Nshan Erganian

Dr. Nshan Erganian wrote this piece in 2004. His mother, Rose (Sarkisian) Erganian passed away on Christmas Day 2009.

1955 was a great year for me, and it left a memory that would last a lifetime. It all happened in my parents' backyard one afternoon as an autumn breeze swayed tree limbs loaded with thousands of colorful maple leaves high above my head.

I was a ten-year-old kid who loved to play baseball and dreamed of being in the major leagues. My fantasy was to just skip all of the usual stops along the way to becoming a major leaguer. There would be no T-ball, Little League, American Legion, or college-level baseball training for me. Even the minor league farm clubs would miss the opportunity of having me in uniform. No siree, it would be straight to the major leagues for this kid whose parents often referred to him as being "quite full of vinegar". That phrase always seemed a little strange to me since my mother never served vinegar at the dinner table.

1955, and many years that followed, was a special time for kids who enjoyed the game of baseball. The spirit of legendary Babe Ruth was captured on just about every vacant lot by kids swinging a "Louisville Slugger" and pounding their baseball mitts. There were a lot of baseball greats in those years. Ted Williams, Brooks Robinson, Hank Aaron, Mickey Mantle, and Roy Campanella, to name a few.

I had some special baseball heroes that I chose to mimic in my "pretend world".

As Joe DiMaggio, the Yankee Clipper, I could blast a baseball deep into the center field stands. My Willie Mays underhand catches of high-fly balls were spectacular.

And, when it came to making a clutch hit to drive in the winning run in the bottom of the ninth inning, who better to emulate than Stan "The Man" Musial of the St. Louis Cardinals? Schucks, I played in so many baseball games during a Saturday afternoon that I thought I had become Lou Gehrig, the "Iron Horse".

On that particular autumn day, I found myself becoming bored with throwing a ball against the brick wall of our house in St. Joseph, Missouri, and shagging the ricochets tightly in the leather pocket of my baseball glove. I really needed a partner to play ball with me, someone to share the "thrill of victory and the agony of defeat." But, there would not be many defeats on that day. Oh no, not for my backyard legends of baseball.

My two teenage sisters, Mary and Carolyn, were usually good for only a few throws of the ball as far as I was concerned. They were more interested in spending their time engaged in more "girlie" things. They preferred to pretend that Pat Boone was actually singing *Love Letters in the Sand* to them, or giggling about how many petticoats they could cram under their poodle skirts. Obviously, they weren't very good candidates for baseball chatter such as, "Hey bitta-bitta, hey bitta-bitta! Come on, fire that hot tomato right down the alley!" My little sister, Roxy, was only five years old, so she was still considered a "minor leaguer".

My father, Nick, was a great fellow, but he was usually busy on weekends trying
to catch up on work around the house, so I decided not to add *play ball with son* onto his "to do" list. Besides, Dad might just figure that if I helped him rake leaves or dig up flower bulbs, he might find some extra time to play ball with me. Whoa! This "Yankee Clipper" was way too smart to get trapped into doing yard work for Dad. I thought there was no one else to play ball with me and I began to cry.

Then I heard a familiar voice say, "Honey, what's the matter? No one to play ball with you?" It was my mother and she had heard my sobbing while she was washing the kitchen windows. She spoke in a soft, consoling voice. "Well, I'd like to play with you. That is, if you don't mind playing with a somewhat rusty baseball player."

Wow! I was shocked, amazed, and spooked! I had never played baseball with my Mom. Shoot, I wasn't even sure Mom knew how to play baseball. After all, she had to be at least thirty years old, and she was a woman, too! For sure, she could cook meals, wash dishes, and change diapers, but could Mom play ball, too? Now, that was a stretch of the imagination for this kid.

I started thinking: *"What the heck, any ball player is better than no ball player."* Ole' Dizzy Dean would have been mighty proud of me. I looked at my mother and blubbered as she gently wiped my glistening eyes. "Okay, Mom, but I don't have a baseball mitt for you."

My mother just smiled and said, "That's okay, I used to catch barehanded when
I played baseball with your uncle and his buddies." Now, if that didn't just about floor me, then nothing would. Really? Mom played baseball with my Uncle Noray?
Gee whiz! That was enough to knock a fella right out of his cleats!

So, the game began. I pitched and Mom was my catcher. I was transformed into a combination of Bob Gibson and Whitey Ford. It didn't really matter if they played for different major league teams. When you're pretending, you can put any players you want on your team.

Well, it didn't take long for the crocodile tears that had streamed down my cheeks to disappear. I was a happy kid and my laughter could be heard coming from our backyard throughout the neighborhood. I would go into an extended windup, look over my shoulder to keep an imaginary runner on base, and then fire the ball to Mom. Oops, I mean the catcher.

She caught every pitch barehanded: the high ones, the low-and-inside ones, my curve ball, and my change-up pitch. Why, she even snagged the wild ones that I threw into the dirt. I must have thrown my mother a hundred pitches, and she didn't muff one of them. And, after every catch of my blazing pitches, Mom would return the ball to me in underhand fashion with just enough of a lob that allowed the ball to easily drop into the pocket of my baseball mitt.

Only once when I burned a fast pitch really high-and-outside did Mom have trouble. Surprisingly, she jumped about two feet off the ground and grabbed the ball with her right hand just before it was about to smash through the window of our garage. Dad would not have been happy to hear the sound of breaking glass. It was a really fantastic catch, and by a mom! However, I noticed that right after the catch my mother was rubbing a finger on her right hand.

"Mom, are you okay?" I timidly asked.

"I'm fine," she said with a slight hesitation. Then she looked at me with a smile on her face and lobbed the ball back to me.

Well, Mom wasn't okay because I noticed that she continued to rub that finger the rest of the afternoon. I had seen sprained fingers before and knew that Mom was going to have a sore finger for a long time. I just didn't realize how long it would linger.

It seemed like we played catch for hours, but who knows? You don't keep track of that stuff when you're enjoying the game. It's the runs, hits, and errors that are the important thing to record when you're playing the "big game" in your backyard.

Our baseball games went on forever on that afternoon in 1955. Just Mom and me, and a thousand, a million, maybe even a gazillion pitches! We finally decided to wind it down as the sun began to fade and the air turned cool.

Mom wrapped her arm around my shoulder as we walked to the house. She didn't say a word, but I knew how much she loved me. I just said, "Thanks, Mom, you're a real pal."

Fifty-two autumns have passed since that day when a ten-year-old and his mom whipped the best talent in the major leagues. I would compete in many more athletic events during those passing years, but none ever came close to matching that backyard game in 1955.

My father passed away a few years ago and I came to realize what a fine man he was. He worked hard to provide for his family, and he really didn't have much spare time to play baseball. Nowadays, I often visit my mother at the family home and take care of the yard that used to serve as my ball diamond. Mom doesn't make it into the yard very often. Many years of life and the onset of arthritis have taken a toll. Now, the spirited thirty-year-old woman who once caught every pitch in the "big game" seems content to sit by her kitchen window that overlooks our make-believe major league stadium. I pause to reflect when I'm working in my mother's yard, especially in the autumn when there is a freshness in the air and those maple leaves turn into brilliant colors. I see my mother sitting at the window, slightly rubbing her finger and smiling at me.

I smile, too...good memories really do last a lifetime.

"BASEBALLS AND PEANUTS" Photo by James Fly

GRANDPA'S GUIDE TO CARING FOR TWIN TODDLERS
(A Spoof) By Nshan Erganian

I waited nearly forty years for that special day. During that span of time, I accumulated knowledge and experience as an educator, consultant, administrator, and business owner. Now, I have reached the pinnacle of my journey. I'm retired!

I now realize that before I can pursue my dreams of fishing, hunting, browsing garage sales, and taking afternoon naps, I still need to direct my talents toward fulfilling one final goal; helping my wife become more efficient in caring for our twin grandchildren. Thus, I am inspired to share my ideas regarding caring for the "little poopers".

I have organized this guide into five areas that seem to encompass my wife's entire day caring for Hope and Chase, our twin grandchildren. The little tykes seem to fall into the following phases:

        A. Waking and Pooping
        B. Nourishment and Grazing
        C. Playtime Torture
        D. Bath Floods
        E. Nap Avoidance

Waking and Pooping:

It seems to me that my wife is doing everything all wrong. Whenever the little ones awake, Marylin eventually asks the key question, "Do we have to go potty?" Wrong approach.

She needs to immediately take control of the situation, especially when the twins are still a little

160

dazed from sleeping. Just give the order, "Okay, you little poopers! Forward march! Hit that potty in double-time, and don't let me see anything left behind!"

Now in the case of the grandson, simply plant his bald little bottom on that cold toilet seat and bark a command, "Fire at will!" The granddaughter, little Hope, can have a seat closer to the floor on the spongy kiddie toilet.

She won't cause a problem because she's probably in a state of shock from watching her twin brother try to obey the earlier command. Warning: be prepared to take evasive action in the event the little boy has difficulty aiming the "cannon". This lack of control can be overcome with the purchase of an inexpensive plastic funnel available at Wal-Mart for about eighty-seven cents, plus three rolls of fifty-foot duct tape.

Simply heat the funnel in a microwave oven for eight to ten seconds. Then, use the duct tape to attach the funnel to the little guy's "Big Bertha". Three rolls of tape should be sufficient, but be careful not to overheat the funnel. Several child advocacy groups will come knocking on your door.

Now, once again, give the command, "Fire at will!" This should produce the desired result. Unless, of course, the little grandson happens to have a playmate whose name *is* Will. In that case, there will likely be problems with the neighbors.

Nourishment and Grazing:

I notice that another of Marylin's problems in caring for Hope and Chase is that she always considers them to be "beautiful little ones" that need love, nurturing, and constant attention. Wrong approach.

Think of the grandchildren much in the same way that ranchers view their cattle—always grazing. Marylin spends a great deal of time preparing food for the twins. I think this is a tremendous waste of human energy, especially since most of it ends up on the floor. I propose an alternative.

Prepare all the food at one time that you expect them to eat during the entire day, say about 10:00 a.m. Yes, that's right. Three or four bowls of Rice Krispies or Fruit Loops, half a dozen eggs, and several chocolate cup cakes. That should keep them stuffed with plenty of energy until they greet their parents at the front door at 4:45 p.m.

I suggest we avoid Grape Nuts and Bran Flakes. Otherwise, the little ones will have to re-visit the section about *Waking and Pooping* on several occasions throughout the day.

The key to being successful with the "nourishment" part of the plan is recognizing that the twins have an obsession with "grazing" for food all day.

So, purchase several head of lettuce and sprinkle them around the house for the kids to enjoy. Lettuce really isn't that messy as long as they chomp on the entire head. Also, it is very healthy and it avoids having to clean up after those M&M's that you thought didn't melt in the hands. Believe me, they do melt under the couch cushions and inside grandpa's slippers.

Playtime Torture:
I notice that my wife exerts huge amounts of energy

doing everything from bouncing balls to pushing tricycles for the grandkids. This can easily be avoided by using an activity that I call *Flying with the Walendos.*

When it's time for the twins to get their fresh air and exercise, simply place them into swings that are equipped with child-restraint safety belts. I realize there is nothing new about swinging children. However, I notice that most grandparents only give the swing a gentle push. This allows the child to enjoy only a few slow passes back and forth until the momentum ceases and the kids scream at the top of their lungs, "Push me higher, grandma, higher, higher, higher, higher!"

I prefer to combine a time and energy-saving method to swinging. Instead of the gentle push, gradually build up the swaying motion until the swing is at a 90-degree angle in relation to the person who is doing the pushing. Then, on the very next push, "Give it your all and send that sucker flying!" The added momentum should catapult the swing into an arc right over the top bar of the swing set. After several loop-de-loops, the swing will return to its usual slow, back and forth motion. This allows a person at least ten minutes before its time to again launch the little ones. This method puts an end to that constant "push me higher" haranguing. You'll know if the twins are enjoying the activity if their eyes become the size of headlights on a semi as they're doing loop-de-loops. A word of caution: Double-check the seat belts prior to the big push. Child advocacy groups may frown on what might appear to be training the little ones for a circus trapeze act.

Bath Floods:

After I helped Marylin bathe the little ones a few times, it occurred to me that there must be a better way to wash all of the carpets than putting two kids into a bath tub with some rubber boats, duckies, and plastic pails. Niagara Falls is beautiful, but not when it's flowing out your front door.

The old saying is that "a person can drown, even in inches of water." My focus on the bath topic reduces the flooding and still protects the little ones. Scuba gear is the answer. Here's how it works:

Simply place a diving mask and a 40-pound self-contained air tank on each child during bath time. The weight of the air tank should anchor the child's rump to the tub, and restrict movements that cause water to splash over the rim and onto the carpet. The air tank should provide at least sixty minutes of oxygen so, even if you're watching Dr. Phil on television, you can still bring the kids to the surface without harm. A word of caution: Do not try to extend your relaxation time to include the Dr. Oz show. That's too much silly advice for anyone in one afternoon, and there's not enough air in the tanks. Child advocacy groups may get a little concerned.

Nap Avoidance:

I've grown tired of parents and grandparents complaining about kids being rowdy and not going to sleep during naptime. My wife usually spends about forty-five minutes easing the grandchildren into this important part of the day. She uses food, toys, and threats as the main method of motivation. Yup, wrong approach. As usual, I have an option.

Sit the little ones on the couch and in a very deep voice announce, "Okay, you little squirts, there's a big monster outside the door who just loves to eat teeny-weeny fingers and toes. So, you better sit still!"

Next, you dig out that ancient VCR stored in the basement and pop in an old videotape of the 1950's western *Red River*. It's a great movie starring

John Wayne, Walter Brennan, Montgomery Cliff, and John Ireland. The grandkids don't care about those "old codgers", but the movie is filled with hundreds of longhorn steers making this cattle drive that runs the entire length of the movie. There are lots of scenes with cattle in dust, cattle grazing, and cattle pooping. And, if there's anything we've learned so far about the grandkids, it's that they love dirt, grazing, and pooping!

Now don't forget about the heads of lettuce from the Nourishment and Grazing Section. It's okay for the grandkids to graze on a few head of lettuce while they're watching *Red River* on that broken-down VCR that keeps skipping past sections of the movie and chewing up the videotape. In fact, that cattle drive takes so long that your little cherubs will probably drift to sleep before John Wayne and Montgomery Cliff have the infamous fistfight during the climax. It's the same ending that adult audiences waited ninety minutes to see on the "big screen" six decades ago.

When the little ones are bloated on lettuce and have drifted into slumber land, it's a good opportunity to straighten up the house before their mom and dad get home. Don't panic. Picking up the toys and pieces of lettuce is a snap if you purchase a "Bob the Builder Mini Bobcat" at Walmart for about $259. The petite model can carry an adult weighing less than one hundred and twenty-five pounds. Larger folks will need the industrial model. It runs about $389, but it can tote a two hundred and forty pound grandpa and it will scoop at least eighty Legos in one pass. A couple of runs through the house and you're ready to be featured in *Better Homes and Gardens*.

The little angels should be awakening from their *Red River* nap about the time their mom and dad come through the door. Now, thanks to you (and the *Grandpa's Guide)*; the kids are clean, rested, and well-fed. No doubt, they'll get a big smile on their faces, run to embrace their parents, and never want to stop clinging to mom and dad's legs screaming, "Please Mommy and Daddy, don't ever leave us again!"

So you see, raising kids isn't really so hard. It's just a matter of being organized, using a little psychology, and wanting to help your spouse.

The Bitter End

Author's note: If you wish to learn more about caring for the grandkids, do not attempt to reach the author at his residence. He will be staying at the local Best Western Inn until things get patched-up with grandma.

SECTION IV

Young Writers
Contest Winners

WHEN JESUS COMES
By Sarah Chevalier, 10th grade

If there is anything I do not know, it is this:
That there be love and hope and joy and peace
On the earth;
For do not these things belong to Heaven?
My soul is weary, my heart downcast.
If I had happiness, it did not last
Till dawn.
I look around and see Pain and fear and sorrow.
My LORD I do not see
His adoration I do not feel.
Blood drips onto the pencil as I write
As bleeding from my heart.
The skies are grey, the day overcast.
The joy I once felt
Is no more; was it ever even there?
Shadows of terror stalk my every step
And I hear the Devil laughing as I stumble
But I'll hold fast God takes care of the humble.
The days drag on without end
With no one faithful to be my friend.
Moans of despair rise up around me
And my voice adds to the chorus in my heart.
If there is anything I do not know, it is this:
That there be love and hope and joy and peace
On the earth;
For do not these things belong to Heaven?
But when Jesus comes – Ah, when Jesus comes!
Then it will be so – For then Heaven and earth
Will be one.

I AM WATER
By McKell Norris, 8th grade

I am from a stream as soft as the moist ground around
me,
To a rushing powerful waterfall,
Dark and mysterious,
Then sitting in the ocean
Alone,
Waiting to strike like a poised cobra
Coming up to high tide
Into a roaring tsunami,
Sweeping away the widow's
Only home.
Building, pets, people,
Bend under my weight and are flattened.
Death and destruction,
All my own doing,
Haunt me like a shadow.
Guilt that weighs a million pounds
Reminds me that this is not who I am.
Not
Who I want to be.
I want to sacrifice for those I hurt.
Evaporating.
Into the clouds.
Becoming.
Changing.
Into a gentle misting rain,
Cleansing the air,
Nourishing the plants,
Quenching the thirsty, and

Filling the empty.
Filling the stream as soft as the moist ground around.
Me.
A place for children to laugh
And play
And pray.
Where the living are refreshed and
I find solace.
Not in the controlling tsunami
Or the dark and powerful waterfall
But in the work of quenching the thirst of the desperate
And being a calm beach or a gentle stream
Or the softly falling
Rain.

THE GIRL IN THE HALLWAY
By Reagan Webster, 8th grade

She's the girl who stares in the mirror and hates what she sees. Many girls feel that way at some point in their life.

She's different.

You see her walking the halls day after day just like everyone else. She never smiles, never laughs. Her head down, her hair a shield, protecting her. She wields no weapons, can't fight back. You watch day after day, it's always the same. You pretend not to notice: as they block her off, as her shield cracks and they rip it to pieces, as they surround her with their own shield, a shield of hurt.

These girls, they wield weapons, and use them with no reason.

She doesn't struggle, can't fight.

They throw their words and pull her hair. These girls in their tight pants, sparkly shoes, and completely perfect hairdos. They laugh their evil laughs, and you look on. You hear their words, feel their poisonous sting. It's not you, though, so why interfere? You hurry to your next class. You dare to look back once. Just once. In that glance you see a girl, crumpled and silently crying in pain as the others walk away. She looks up, and her eyes meet yours.

You could do something. You could. Her eyes are full of hurt as she gathers her things. You turn away and hurry to class. You can't be late. You leave the girl alone. Alone to hurt. What was that you saw as you rushed away? Were those scars on her wrists?

When she goes home, it will happen again. She'll stare at the beautiful girl in the mirror, and she'll see an imperfect, disgraceful, ugly monster that houses her heart. No one notices her. She'll be crying so hard, she can't see. Then she'll reach for the scissors in a place she knows by heart. She'll open the blade and slice her wrists. She won't even wince at the pain. She'll stare at the blood, and smile, but the tears will still flow. She's not perfectly made-up like those girls with the sparkly shoes. She knows she deserves it all.

She'll remember your face. The other person in the hallway today. The person who saw it all and walked away. More proof she deserves the pain. So she'll slice again, and smear her paint in circles on her canvas, already dry with previous paintings.

She'll smile a smile that's hard to read. Full of pain, but relief as well. She can escape her feelings this way. No one else can hurt her in this place. She wonders, as she slices again, if life is better on the other side. Will it be dark and scary? Or warm and welcoming? When she decides, there's no going back. No one understands her. Any place must be better than here. When they find her they will wonder why it happened. Will the other girls feel guilty?

Could you have stopped it? If you had done something, maybe she would have stopped paint-ing. A new picture added to her canvas every day. Maybe you could have been friends. You'll never know. You might have stopped her hurting, put an end to the pain, if only you'd spoken up. You could have done something.

But now she's gone.

Did you even know her name?

A Message From the Authors:

Thank you for taking the time to read our book.
We would be honored if you would consider
leaving a review for it on Amazon.

Check out these titles from

Amazing Things Press

Time Lost: Teenage Survivalist II by Julie L. Casey

Keeper of the Mountain by Nshan Erganian

Rare Blood Sect by Robert L. Justus

Evoloving by James Fly

Survival In the Kitchen by Sharon Boyle

Stop Beating the Dead Horse by Julie L. Casey

In Daddy's Hands by Julie L. Casey

The Boy Who Loved the Sky by Donna E. Hart

Amazing Things Press

www.amazingthingspress.com

www.ingramcontent.com/pod-product-compliance
Lightning Source LLC
Chambersburg PA
CBHW060813120626
46557CB00001B/205